A Journey into Ireland's Literary Revival

R. Todd Felton

ArtPlace Series

ROARING FORTIES
PRESS

Roaring Forties Press
Berkeley, California

Roaring Forties Press
1053 Santa Fe Avenue
Berkeley, California 94706

Copyright © 2007 by R. Todd Felton
Printed in Hong Kong

ISBN 0-9766706-7-4
ISBN 978-0976670674

Library of Congress Cataloging-in-Publication Data
Felton, R. Todd, 1969-
  A journey into Ireland's literary revival / R. Todd Felton.
      p. cm. -- (ArtPlace series)
  Includes bibliographical references and index.
  ISBN 978-0-9766706-7-4 (pbk. : alk. paper)
 1. Literary landmarks--Ireland. 2. Authors, Irish--Homes and haunts--Ireland. 3. English literature--Irish
authors--History and criticism. 4. Ireland--Intellectual life--20th century. 5. Ireland--Intellectual life--
19th century. 6. Ireland--Description and travel. I. Title.
  PR8731.F46 2007
  820.9'9415--dc22

                                                                                    2006103434

Cover: *Howth and Ireland's Eye.* Courtesy of the Library of Congress (LC-DIG-ppmsc-09883).

To Chris, Tim, and Liam

Contents

Preface and Acknowledgments

I did not have to wait long to witness the Irish gift of storytelling. Mere hours after landing at Shannon Airport and driving out to the village of Gort in County Galway, I was sitting with a group attending the Lady Gregory Society's Autumn Gathering. Among the scholars was a woman whose father's friend had been the undertaker in Gort, where William Butler Yeats had his summer house and was prone to wandering the countryside deep into the night. She told me a story she'd heard from her father. In addition to caring for the dead and bereaved in the town, the undertaker also ran a taxi service using his trap and pony (a type of carriage drawn by a pony). One night the weather turned nasty, and the undertaker battened down all the doors and went to bed. In the middle of the night, he and his wife were awakened by someone pounding on the door, fit to knock it down. A little frightened, the undertaker stuck his head out the window. Seeing who it was, he called back to his wife, "Ah, sure. It's only that mad Yeats, looking for a ride home."

Everywhere I went on that trip, people were happy to help me. On the Aran Islands, where I arrived on the 6 p.m. ferry in the gathering dusk without a place to stay, Vilma Conneely, the owner of the Tig Congaile bed-and-breakfast, took me in. When she heard what I was there for, she happily shared stories of a Japanese theater company that had stayed with her for two weeks on the island of Inis Meáin to get the feel of its "atmosphere" for a production of J. M. Synge's *The Playboy of the Western World*. She also informed me that her husband was a direct descendant of Máirtín MacDonnchadha, the man who served as Synge's personal guide to Inis Meáin. Another man I met in a small hotel in County Mayo pulled a chair up to my breakfast table to make sure I knew the story of Coranna the horse.

It is this bounty of stories that makes writing a book like this both difficult and easy. Deciding what to put in and what to leave out was certainly the greatest challenge. A study like this offers a unique—but, I hope, not idiosyncratic—

portrait. There are some obvious missing faces in this class picture, however. For instance, James Joyce is not fully covered here, for a variety of reasons, the most persuasive of which is that he himself did not want to be included. Although he was present for parts of the Irish Literary Revival and met most of the central figures, he avoided the entanglements and restrictions that collaboration with them would have entailed.

In addition, some locations associated with these writers receive scant or no attention here. Because this book is intended to be a pleasant traveling companion and not an exhaustive academic study, I have tried to include only the most interesting and representative anecdotes. I have also included, for the most part, only events that happened within Ireland. I did, however, take some liberties with the rather arbitrary time frame set for the Irish Literary Revival. Although Yeats published *The Tower* two years after Sean O'Casey's *The Plough and the Stars*, I discuss poems from it because they pertain to Thoor Ballylee, Yeats's treasured home.

Many people helped this book come to fruition. My first thanks go to Sighle Meehan, Sheila O'Donnellan, Ronnie O'Gorman, Lois Tobin, and the rest of the Lady Gregory Society for graciously including me in their Autumn Gathering. The highlight of that gathering was, for me, meeting Michael Yeats and Ben Kennedy, and I thank both for their welcoming spirit and generosity. I also want to thank Peggy McCarty-O'Brien for her generous Irish hospitality, Richard Fallis and Robert Meagher for their advice, and Nancy Rosenwald for her suggestions. I alos wish to thank Colin Smythe, the National Library, Allison D'Arcy, Art O'Sullivan, and Old Irish Images for their assistance in identifying images and, in many cases, bestowing permissions. As always, I want to thank Deirdre Greene and Nigel Quinney for their faith. My sons, Liam and Tim, and my wife, Chris, have made writing this book fun, and being done with it even more fun.

A Journey into
Ireland's
Literary Revival

Chapter 1
The Irish Literary Revival
A Geography of the Public and the Private

Dawn on the Aran Island of Inis Meáin.

On the night of April 2, 1902, the Irish National Theatre Society presented two plays to a packed house at St. Teresa's Total Abstinence Hall on Dublin's Clarendon Street. Although the first of these plays, *Deirdre*, a retelling of an ancient Irish myth involving love and loyalty, entertained the audience, it was the next play, *Cathleen Ni Houlihan*, that gripped those in the hall.

Set in the small western village of Killala, where French forces landed to aid the Irish in their 1798 uprising against the British, the play depicts a family preparing for the eldest son's wedding. When an old woman enters the cottage and tells the story of how her "four green fields" were taken from her, the young groom is so entranced that he pledges to fight, and if necessary die, to regain her lands. As the crone leaves the family's tiny cottage, her youth and beauty are restored by the young man's pledge to die for her, and she is transformed into a radiant queen—Cathleen Ni Houlihan, a mythical symbol of Irish nationalism.

Although the audience was well aware of what happened during that doomed rebellion of 1798 (the British eventually crushed the resistance), the combination of the strikingly tall and beautiful nationalist Maud Gonne in the title role and the rousing monologues penned by poet William Butler Yeats so stirred passions among the gathered Dubliners that they stood singing patriotic songs as the curtain fell.

This one night in the theater was a milestone in the history of Ireland's Literary Revival, a bold and remarkably influential cultural movement that germinated in the 1890s and blossomed in the 1900s and 1910s, before beginning to fade in the 1920s. The Revival drew together many of Ireland's finest writers and scholars in an effort to rejuvenate an Irish literary and cultural tradition that been subverted by hundreds of years of British political domination. The performance of *Cathleen Ni Houlihan* in April 1902 exemplified much about the Revival's agenda: a play written by Irish writers celebrating Irish history, acted by Irish actors, and presented in an Irish city to an Irish audience.

Yet, to describe the play purely in those terms may give a misleading and oversimplified impression of the

Actress Maud Gonne starring as the crone—soon to turn radiant queen—in *Cathleen Ni Houlihan*.

ambitions that inspired the Revival. Its members sought not just to reanimate a long-dormant tradition but to develop a new and distinct national cultural identity for Ireland, one that would throw off the unflattering stereotypes developed under British rule and replace them with a rich and colorful fabric woven both from Celtic mythology and from the unvarnished experiences of ordinary Irish men and women. The Revival celebrated Ireland's history and the spirit of its people, but it also looked with unflinching honesty at the conditions of life in the isolated villages and bustling cities of contemporary Ireland. The members of the Revival were not propagandists but artists, and the Ireland they portrayed was beautiful but full of complexities, blemishes, and contradictions. This contradictory nature was mirrored in the Revivalists themselves, many of whom were wealthy, Protestant, Anglo-Irish landowners, even though most of their creative work dealt with the struggles of poor, Catholic, Irish tenant farmers and laborers.

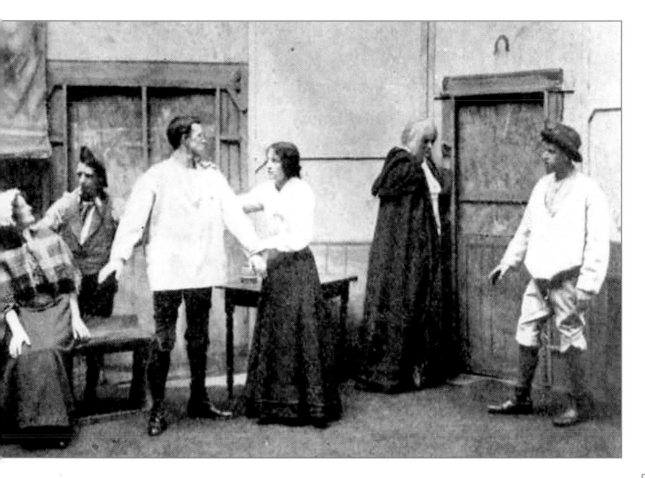

Appropriately enough for a movement that embraced such contradictions while straddling art and politics, the history of the Revival is a tale told through both contemplative, private moments and rousing public spectacles. These very different moods were two sides of the same coin; indeed, they inspired each other. For instance, the artistic journey that led to the stirring performance of *Cathleen Ni Houlihan* on a spring

What's in a Name?

The Irish Literary Revival was many things to many people—and thus it had a wide variety of names. Some borrowed the name of one of Yeats's books and called the movement the Celtic Twilight, especially during its early years, when much of the literature it produced focused on Celtic legends. Others referred to it as the Celtic Movement, the Celtic Renaissance, or the Celtic School.

These names were used by critics and disciples alike to underline that the movement was interested not in contemporary "Irish culture" (which at the time

Many places in Ireland have both a Gaelic and an Anglicized name. The Aran island of Inis Mór, for instance, is also known as Inishmoor.

was essentially British culture imported from London) but in a "Celtic culture" that had its roots in a mythology and history that stretched back thousands of years. This was an important distinction to the members of the Revival, many of whom were Protestant, Anglo-Irish landowners but wished to make it clear that their hopes lay with an independent Ireland of the future.

As the movement widened its focus to become not just a campaign to recover a lost literature but a crusade to create a new voice for a new nation, its adherents began moving away from the term *Celtic* and toward *Irish*. Over the years, the names Irish Literary Renaissance, Irish Cultural Revival, and (probably the most common name today) Irish Literary Revival came into use, explicitly proclaiming the movement's goal of reviving an indigenous culture and building a new cultural tradition. The "Revival" (to use the short form that is often employed in this book) should not be confused with the Gaelic Revival (or Irish Language Revival), which was primarily an effort to teach the Gaelic language and promote traditional Gaelic singing, dancing, and sports.

evening in 1902 had begun five years earlier and hundred of miles away, during a rainy afternoon conversation between friends over tea.

*   *   *

On that afternoon in the west of Ireland in 1897, Lady Augusta Gregory, the wealthy widow of a County Galway landowner, and a shy, awkward poet from Dublin, William Butler Yeats, sat next to a roaring fire, looking out of large windows lashed by wind and rain, and decided that the time had come for Ireland to have its own theater. A few days later, together with playwright Edward Martyn, they retired to the sylvan quiet of Gregory's estate, Coole Park, and wrote to anybody who might support their dramatic ambitions. "We will show that Ireland is not the home of buffoonery and of easy sentiment, as it has been represented, but the home of an ancient idealism," their letter declared. "We are confident of the support of all Irish people, who are weary of misrepresentation, in carrying out a work that is outside all the political questions that divide us."

Over the next few years, the widow and the poet grew to be close collaborators as they not only championed the idea of Ireland's own theater company—what became known as the Irish National Theatre Society—but also became its producers and playwrights. *Cathleen Ni Houlihan*, destined for a boisterous Dublin reception, was one of the plays written in the tranquility of Coole Park. The enthusiasm that greeted *Cathleen* helped generate the momentum that led to the founding of the Abbey Theatre, which was for many the public center of the Irish Literary Revival.

Just as the story of *Cathleen* moves from intimate spaces (the peasants' cottage) to public stages

(the battlefields of the 1798 uprising and the vast expanse of Irish cultural myth), so this book journeys between the private spaces where writers wrestled with what it meant to be Irish and the public stages on which many of the concerns and theories of the Revival were acted out. *A Journey into Ireland's Literary Revival* visits the houses where the poets and playwrights lived and retraces their steps through the woods and along the cliffs to the intimate spots of nature that inspired them. The book also explores the public spaces of the Revival—the stages and streets of Dublin and other cities as well as the public monuments and landmarks that commemorate the Revival's achievements.

Out of the Ashes of Politics

The Irish Literary Revival emerged out of the ashes of a political failure: a scandal that toppled one of Ireland's most beloved politicians, Charles Stewart Parnell, in

Charles Stewart Parnell's crusade for Home Rule inspired fierce passions, as shown in this 1890 engraving of Parnell addressing a hostile crowd.

7

An Claidheamh Soluis was published by the Gaelic League to promote Irish culture.

1890. Parnell had been a leading voice for Home Rule, or political separation from British authority. A member of Parliament from County Meath, the charismatic Parnell electrified the countryside with his oratory, as Irish scholar Ulick O'Connor describes:

Parnell was the first of the ruling caste to speak for the whole nation in a constitutional crusade. He epitomized the new Irishman and sent waves of regeneration through the people that hastened the process of recognition of the national being. It was the exhilaration and elation of this period that excited the imagination of writers and artists, and, as in the case of the Elizabethan age, led to the creation of significant literature.

Unfortunately, just as Parnell seemed poised to accomplish what various armed uprisings had failed to do, he was derailed, not by politics or armed violence, but by social intrigue. In 1890, Captain William O'Shea filed for divorce from his wife, Katharine, and identified Parnell as a third party in the suit. As his long-term affair with the woman the media called "Kitty" came to light ("Kitty" was not only short for "Katharine" but also slang for "prostitute"), Parnell faced a torrent of public censure from a staunchly Catholic society that condemned such relationships. Although he eventually married Katharine, the scandal robbed Parnell of his influence in the country, and he eventually lost control of the Irish Parliamentary Party.

With the departure of Parnell from the national scene, many of his former supporters redirected their efforts from politics to cultural activities, working to create opportunities for the men and women of Ireland to express their "Irishness." Whereas progress in the political realm seemed impossible, real advances in the realm of culture appeared within reach. Some even argued that cultural independence was the first step to political independence.

At the forefront of this new shift toward cultural activities stood Douglas Hyde, the son of a County Roscommon rector. Hyde's collections of Gaelic folk poems "set the style of the literary renaissance," notes Ulick O'Connor. "The direct translations enabled the writers to get the rhythm of Irish language spoken into their ears. Some of them would return to the source by learning Irish." The three volumes—*Beside the Fire* (1890), *The Love Songs of Connacht* (1893), and *Religious Songs of Connacht* (1906)—contain the very language and themes that would later surface in the poetry of William Butler Yeats, in the folk myths of Lady Gregory, and in the dialogue of J. M. Synge's plays. For example, Synge's 1904 drama about a woman who loses all the men of her family to the ocean, *Riders to the Sea*, echoes the tragic tenor of Hyde's translation of a traditional lyric, "My Grief on the Sea":

> *My grief on the sea,*
> *How the waves of it roll!*
> *For they heave between me*
> *And the love of my soul!*

Hyde also contributed to the Irish Literary Revival in his role as a founder and the leader of the Gaelic League. Established on July 31, 1893, the league took as its mission the restoration of Gaelic to its former place on the tongues of the Irish people. Use of Gaelic had been on the decline throughout the nineteenth century, in part because Britain had decreed in 1831 that all government-funded schools would teach only in English, and in part because of the economic necessity of trading in English. In a seminal speech of 1892 to the National Literary Society called "The Necessity for De-Anglicizing Ireland," Hyde maintained that the only path to political freedom for Ireland was to strengthen the country's awareness of its indigenous culture. Relearning Ireland's native tongue, he argued, should be a central part of an overall strategy for achieving political freedom. His speech was nothing less than an educational call to arms.

W. B. Yeats in 1900, painted by his father.

Lady Gregory's own contributions to the Irish Literary Revival have only recently begun receiving the critical attention they deserve.

mixes with the magical. The stories deal with legendary beauties, seaside ghosts, and hosts of fairies riding across the landscape. Yeats's reputation as a leading scholar of folktales was cemented by publication of two poetry collections, *The Rose* and *The Wind among the Reeds*, which featured many of the same themes and imagery. *The Celtic Twilight* was so influential that many people began to use the title to describe a fledgling group of writers that, following Yeats's lead, was rediscovering the richness of Ireland's literary culture. Various members of this group debated what their common ambitions should be, but Yeats was in no doubt that his goal was, in scholar Robert Tracy's words, to "provide the free Ireland of the future with pride in a glorious past." As Yeats explained in "To Ireland in the Coming Times," the final poem in his 1893 collection *The Rose*,

> *Know, that I would accounted be*
> *True brother of a company*
> *That sang, to sweeten Ireland's wrong,*
> *Ballad and story, rann and song.*

In all, Yeats wrote thirteen collections of poetry; nearly two dozen plays, many of them experimental; and a remarkable variety of prose, including three autobiographies and a wealth of literary criticism. In addition, he lectured often and widely on subjects ranging from poetry and drama to Eastern mysticism. When not writing, Yeats was frequently in the public's eye as a director of the Irish National Theatre Society (later, the Abbey Theatre).

To accomplish this "de-Anglicizing," branches of the Gaelic League were set up around the country to provide instruction in Gaelic, organize a wide variety of events and cultural activities, and rally political support. By the early twentieth century, about five hundred Gaelic League branches were spread across Ireland. The Gaelic League also published its own weekly newspaper, *An Claidheamh Soluis*, and helped sponsor artists dedicated to reviving Celtic folk arts such as knitting and weaving.

Singing to Sweeten Ireland's Wrong

Against this backdrop of an energetic campaign to reclaim the nation's self-identity, William Butler Yeats began introducing Irish readers to ancient Celtic stories that were on the brink of being lost. In his 1893 collection of poems, myths, legends, and ghost stories, *The Celtic Twilight*, Yeats conjures up an Ireland that is as poetic as it is beautiful, a land where the mythic is merely a shade beyond the truth and the mundane

The relationship between Irish politics and Irish art during the years of the Revival was often intimate but rarely straightforward, as Yeats himself typified. His work could be explicitly political, and when Ireland finally won independence from Britain in the early 1920s, it was no surprise that he became a senator in

James Joyce

Although a contemporary of many of the figures in the Irish Literary Revival, Ireland's greatest fiction writer was very much not a part of the movement. James Joyce, born in Dublin in 1882, had lived in various locations around the city all his life and was attending University College when he went to see *Casadh an tSugan* and *Diarmuid and Grania*, put on by the Irish Literary Theatre in 1901. He reacted to the production with contempt in his essay "The Day of the Rabblement," in which he proposed that the Irish Literary Theatre's reluctance to take on the modern plays of Europe limited it: "The Irish Literary Theatre must now be considered the property of the rabblement of the most belated race in Europe." He saw its mission of promoting Irish art as misguided and essentially hopeless.

Despite such misgivings, Joyce was intrigued by some of the Revival's leading members. He managed to meet both Yeats and George Russell (known as AE) in 1902. He waited for AE outside his Dublin house and, after AE returned late at night, knocked on the door and asked to come in. The two writers talked until four in the morning. Although AE was impressed with Joyce's intelligence, he was also struck by his arrogance. On Joyce's side, he thought enough of AE to leave his poems and epiphanies (short prose sketches around a sudden moment of insight) with the poet when he left for Paris in December 1902. AE also read the original manuscript for *Stephen Hero* (which later became *A Portrait of the Artist as a Young Man*) and suggested that Joyce write stories for *The Irish Homestead*. The magazine published three of Joyce's stories in the fall of 1904: "The Sisters," "Eveline," and "After the Race." All eventually became part of *Dubliners*, Joyce's famous collection of short stories, which was modeled after George Moore's story collection, *The Untilled Field*.

Before Joyce left for Paris, he met Yeats in the street in Dublin. They went to a café, where, according to Yeats, Joyce peppered him with questions about why he was wasting his talent. When it was time to leave, Joyce asked how old Yeats was, then replied with a sniff, "I thought as much. I have met you too late. You are too old."

the national assembly of the new state. Yet, while at some times he presented his art as a servant of politics, at other times he would declare that art should serve no master but art. In 1923, he became the first Irishman to win the Nobel Prize for Literature.

Yeats's closest friend and most important supporter was Lady Gregory, whose own contributions to the Revival were highly influential. Inspired by Hyde and Yeats, Lady Gregory traveled her beloved Connacht listening to the stories told by the *seanachi* (traveling professional storytellers) and the local tenant farmers. Her retellings of these myths were published in eight volumes, two of Irish saga and romance and six of folklore and translations. Then, when her Abbey Theatre needed new material, she turned to writing plays, more than forty in all. The vast majority of these were immensely popular "peasant comedies," such as *Spreading the News* and *The Workhouse Ward*, which were staple fare at the Abbey for many decades.

Synge's career was short, lasting less than ten years, but he had a major impact on Ireland's literary world.

Another writer for the Abbey Theatre and the third member of the triumvirate that ruled over its early years was John Millington Synge. The son of a Protestant landowner, Synge struggled early to make his way as an artist. Happiest among the barren heaths of Wicklow, south of Dublin, but itching to make his artistic mark, Synge met up with Yeats in Paris in December 1896, where the elder writer advised the eager young man to go to the Aran Islands, off the west coast of Ireland, to find both inspiration and stories. A year and a half later Synge did just that. The experience helped him craft lilting, Gaelic-inflected dialogue based on the everyday speech of Irish peasants. He also penned a landmark study of the people of the Aran Islands, as well as a set of five plays that changed the landscape of Irish drama. The most famous of these, *The Playboy of the Western World*, provoked riots at its January 1907 opening for the frankness of its language and the violence of its patricidal theme.

Edward Martyn and George Moore, writers and cousins, also played important roles in the Revival. Martyn, a devout Catholic living in a Gothic castle in Galway near Lady Gregory's Coole Park, helped establish the Irish Literary Theatre, wrote plays, and eventually formed his own theater group in Dublin. Martyn was also responsible for bringing the talents and energies of George Moore into the movement. Moore, who had been making a living as a novelist and art critic in London, was recruited to help produce the first plays of the Irish Literary Theatre. He then moved back to Ireland and jumped into the cultural resurgence, determined to find ways to be involved. He landed on a project to write short stories set in his western Ireland home of County Mayo. Although his initial plan to translate all the stories into Gaelic for publication in newspapers was derailed by the Catholic Church, many stories were published by the Gaelic League in side-by-side translations under the title *An-tUr Ghort*. Moore later revised them and published them in English as *The Untilled Field*, marking what many consider to be the birth of the modern Irish short story.

In Dublin, other voices were destined to make their contributions to the growing chorus of Irish literature. One of Yeats's close friends from art school was George Russell, a poet and painter who used the pen name of AE. In addition to writing, he mentored young Dublin writers and helped design theater scenery. AE was also instrumental in Horace Plunkett's agricultural cooperative to help beleaguered Irish farmers make a living, serving as editor of *The Irish Homestead*. Among the fresh new voices he brought to the weekly newspaper was a little-known young man by the name of James Joyce.

By the mid-1920s, the Literary Revival had lost some of its counterculture force. Its leading voice, Yeats, was now a senator in the Irish Free State. Lady

County Galway
The Aran Islands
County Mayo
County Sligo
County Wicklow
Dublin

SCOTLAND
Coleraine
NORTHERN IRELAND
Belfast
Sligo
Armagh
Castlebar
Cavan
IRELAND
Irish Sea
Athlone
Galway
Atlantic Ocean
Dublin
WALES
Wicklow
Limerick
Kilkenny
Tipperary
Wexford
Waterford
Killarney
Cork
N

Gregory was busy raising her grandchildren at Coole Park. Synge was dead. The Abbey Theatre was a state-subsidized institution, and many of the actors who had made it famous had left for other stages.

But just when it seemed that the Revival had run out of fresh voices, the Abbey Theatre staged a series of plays by Sean O'Casey, which revitalized Irish literature and, once again, inspired rioting. O'Casey's "Dublin Trilogy" (*The Shadow of a Gunman, Juno and the Paycock,* and *The Plough and the Stars*) portrayed the darker sides of cherished chapters in Irish history, such as the 1916 Easter Rising and the war with Britain for independence, and enjoyed tremendous success.

But the Abbey's renaissance was brief. When the theater rejected his next play, O'Casey left Ireland for England. Thereafter, the Abbey settled into a long era of

Yeats wrote of Thoor Ballylee: "Here beside a little stream, I write poetry and think of nothing else."

comfortable mediocrity. Yeats, without Synge and Lady Gregory to spur him on, turned to more personal themes in his poetry. The Revival was over.

Dreaming in Ireland

This book follows the course of the Irish Literary Revival not only literally but also metaphorically, moving from the shadows and brooding silences of cottages and country houses in the west of the country to the floodlit and sometimes rowdy public spaces of Dublin.

The story starts in the intimate setting of County Galway, where so many of the early connections took place: the cozy room at Doorus House where Lady Gregory and Yeats discussed the idea of a national theater; the secret spot by Coole Lake where Yeats counted swans; the house where Lady Gregory hosted so many literary lions; and Yeats's castlelike tower, Thoor Ballylee, where he wrote some of his most introspective and powerful poetry.

Chapter 3 travels to the most remote section of Ireland, the granite-strewn islands known as Inis Mór, Inis Meáin, and Inis Oirr. The Gaeltacht (pure Gaelic-speaking) culture of the hardy islanders appealed to many of the

Revival writers, serving as both symbol and substance of the Celtic culture that the writers committed themselves to preserving. Although Lady Gregory, Yeats, Hyde, and Martyn all visited the islands, it is Synge's account of three of his four summers on the Aran Islands that best portrays the joys and hardships of life among the islanders.

A variant of that same culture could be found back on the mainland, just to the north in the large western county of Mayo. Not far from the geographic center of the county stands the ruined shell of a grand house. With its Italian plasterwork and ornate iron railings, Moore Hall was home to one of the Revival's most flamboyant figures. Playwright, art critic, novelist, and short-story writer George Moore found in the surrounding countryside the raw material for his tales of narrow-minded clerics and hardscrabble farmers faced with no good choices. The bleak and often desolate coasts of County Mayo also provided the settings for two of the Revival's most provocative plays. *Cathleen Ni Houlihan* is set in the northern coastal town of Killala, while the Mullet peninsula provided the isolation needed for *The Playboy of the Western World*.

Just north of Moore's County Mayo is County Sligo, where Yeats spent parts of his childhood. A beguiling and often breathtaking mixture of grassy plains, pristine lakes, and majestic mountains, County Sligo is a perfect setting for Yeats's stories of fairy folk and drew Yeats throughout his life, inspiring one of his best-known poems, "The Lake Isle of Innisfree." In fact, the green fields near the granite cliffs of Ben Bulben were so dear to Yeats that he asked to be buried there, in the tiny churchyard of Drumcliff. The town of Sligo has done much to preserve Yeats's legacy and is the home of the Yeats Centre and the Yeats Summer Institute, current hotspots of scholarship on the Revival.

This book then journeys to the other side of the country, to County Wicklow, which lies along the coast south of Dublin. It was here, in a landscape of moors and mountains, heather and gorse, that J. M. Synge spent his childhood afternoons, often in the company of the tinkers and travelers whose voices he was later to incorporate into his work. Many of the towns and villages of Wicklow have changed little since Synge's time.

This book concludes, appropriately enough, in the bustling streets and public spaces of Ireland's political and cultural capital, Dublin. In cold, drafty rented halls, in literary salons held in plush Georgian houses, in the sometimes boisterous auditoriums of state-funded theaters, and in the marble-clad lobby of the General Post Office, where poets and scholars joined in a rebellion against an empire, the Revival made its work known to a Dublin public that was, by turns, deeply moved and morally outraged. Dublin was home not only to the Abbey Theatre but also to many of the Revival writers. Yeats, Synge, O'Casey, Moore, and AE all lived at various times in the city, and their legacy is still celebrated on both sides of the River Liffey in museums, galleries, and pubs.

The journey charted in the following chapters is one from west to east, from the private to the public, across an island that is as varied as it is striking. This voyage features a group of characters colorful enough to form the cast of a play: the intense and occasionally awkward poet in the black velvet jacket and bow tie, the matriarch playing host to young writers and her own literary ambitions, the quiet young man jotting down overheard snippets of dialogue and tall tales, and the flamboyant man of letters gadding about town in search of a sense of purpose. Diverse though they are, each of these characters was involved in the same drama, the same quest to create from the myths of the past, the struggles of the present, and the hopes for the future a literature—and a culture—that is authentically Irish.

Chapter 2

County Galway
Home among the Swallows

Three of Ireland's winners of the Nobel Prize for Literature have viewed these Coole Park steps as the gateway to a special literary retreat.

The Irish Literary Revival had its roots in County Galway, in the center of the western province of Connacht. Galway comprises more than two thousand square miles of broken limestone, turloughs (seasonal lakes that rise and fall with the water table), and green fields, and twelve hundred miles of craggy coastline. Its largest city and capital, Galway City, sits at the foot of Galway Bay and is a comparative metropolis of seventy thousand people.

East Galway offers pastures and rolling hills, while the Aran Islands, at the head of Galway Bay, are thickly crusted with stone. Hedged in on the south by the tremendous limestone ridge known as the Burren and on the north by the surreal landscapes of Connemara, County Galway has a landscape that both nurtures and inspires.

This diverse countryside has an impressive literary history, in many cases inspired by or intimately connected to the landscape. Stirred by the peaceful beauty of Coole Park and by his house-cum-poetic symbol, Thoor Ballylee, Yeats wrote some of his best-known poetry in County Galway. It was also here, in conversations over tea or around the dinner table, that many of the plans for the Literary Revival were laid. Coole Park, Tullira Castle, Doorus House, Thoor Ballylee—the names of Galway's houses are as poetic as the works conceived in them. Outside, lakes appear and disappear, fourteenth-century towers of gray stone stand next to clear running streams, and bayside villages are wreathed in fog.

At the Center: Coole Park

It is no coincidence that many of the locations described in this chapter are clustered around one estate—Lady Gregory's Coole Park. A widow, Lady Gregory opened her home to the major figures in Irish literary and cultural life at the turn of the century, and nearly all came. Nobel laureates George Bernard Shaw and William Butler Yeats enjoyed extended stays there, with Yeats making it his summer home for many years. Playwrights John Millington Synge and Sean O'Casey appreciated Lady Gregory's generous hospitality, while painters Jack Yeats and Augustus John found much in the surrounding scenery to inspire them.

But this was over the course of many years. Much of the early activity actually took place around Coole Park, at planned and chance meetings where visionary minds met with generous spirits and plans were hatched. Coole Park's neighbors included Edward Martyn's Tullira Castle and the Count de Basterot's Doorus House, which were the initial attractions to the

Coole House in 1887, just seven years after Lady Augusta Gregory arrived as the new mistress and a decade before it would become the center of the Irish Literary Revival.

area for men such as Yeats and Douglas Hyde. But Lady Gregory's house soon eclipsed the others as the central gathering place where intellectuals could discuss culture and literature in an intimate setting.

Among the Many:
Lady Gregory's Childhood at Roxborough

Isabella Augusta Persse's journey from her birthplace at her father's estate of ❶ Roxborough, near the town of Loughrea, to her position as Lady Gregory of Coole Park may have been a short one geographically (the two houses were only seven miles apart), but it was in many ways an epic trek. At Roxborough, she was thought of as the plain, dutiful daughter whose destiny was not to marry but to stay at home and serve her brothers. At Coole Park, she was the wife of an admired former governor of Ceylon and respected local politician. In one house, she was restricted in her activities and limited in her life options. In the other, she became one of the most influential figures in Irish cultural history.

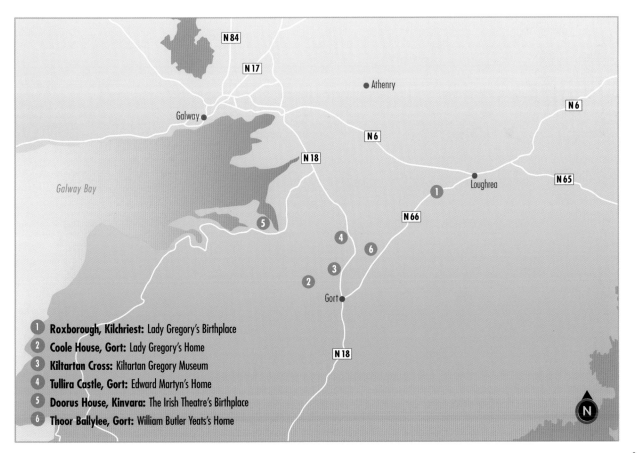

❶ **Roxborough, Kilchriest:** Lady Gregory's Birthplace
❷ **Coole House, Gort:** Lady Gregory's Home
❸ **Kiltartan Cross:** Kiltartan Gregory Museum
❹ **Tullira Castle, Gort:** Edward Martyn's Home
❺ **Doorus House, Kinvara:** The Irish Theatre's Birthplace
❻ **Thoor Ballylee, Gort:** William Butler Yeats's Home

Roxborough, where Lady Gregory grew up.

She very nearly didn't make it out of infancy, however. Augusta was born in the early hours of March 15, 1852, into a "big house" that was big in more than one way: she was one of sixteen children under the same roof. As she relates in her autobiography, *Seventy Years*, her mother had little affection to spare:

> *At the midnight hour between the fourteenth and the fifteenth of March 1852 . . . a little girl was born at Roxborough that is in Connacht. She was the fifth daughter of her mother, and there were two stepdaughters also in the house. And*

although her mother had four sons of her own, besides a stepson, she liked boys better than girls and wished for more sons than daughters, and so was sorry that this was not a boy. Yet when, according to the old nurse's story, this little-welcomed girl had nearly gone out with but a breath of the world's air, being laid aside and forgotten for a while in the quilt of covering, the mother said that she would have been sorry for such a loss, because the other children would have been disappointed at not having a new baby to play with.

With such a start, it is not surprising that Augusta looked for ways to escape. Her mother's combination of piety and disdain literally put the fear of God into her. Endeavoring to save her soul from eternal damnation, Augusta turned to religion. Her mother and sisters were respectable Protestants, even occasionally practicing evangelism on their Catholic neighbors. Although Augusta never took this step, she did resort to daily prayer and earnest living according to the Protestant faith. That is, until literature came into the house.

At Christmas one year, a box arrived with books for the children to choose as presents. Augusta's older sister chose the *Chambers Encyclopedia of English Literature* because it was the largest and best of the books, but for Augusta it held another attraction. When her sister left it on the drawing room table and Augusta was able to read it, she was hooked. She finished it quickly and went back to reread her favorites again and again. The Bible moved over to make room for literature—a shared arrangement that would last for the rest of her life.

Augusta had an active mind and an occasionally rebellious spirit. Some of this was instilled by her Irish nurse, Mary Sheridan, who told her many of the stories she would later collect and publish. Her rebellion also showed in acts like using money she was given for learning Sunday school lessons to buy books celebrating the Fenian uprisings of 1867.

At a cricket party at Roxborough in 1877, Augusta met a neighbor, Sir William Gregory, who had served as the governor of Ceylon for five years. Because one of her brothers was considering a journey there, she and Sir William spent the afternoon talking about his experiences. An invitation to dinner at a mutual friend's house followed, and finally there was a chaperoned visit to Sir William's nearby home, Coole House.

Perhaps the most telling sign of Sir William's budding feelings for Augusta was that, after her visit to Coole Park, he amended his will to include her: when he died, she could choose any six books she wanted from his well-stocked library. Fortunately, he did not die then, she muses in *Seventy Years*; it would not have been an easy choice to make. A friend of her brother's described Coole as "a house showing a fine intellectual tradition . . . the library with its rich collection of books," and had said "with what seemed a flight of fancy, 'That is the only house I have seen in the county that would make a right setting for you.'"

However, romance had to wait. Augusta's father died in 1878, leaving the estate to his oldest son, Dudley, and forcing his wife to relocate to an apartment in Dublin's Merrion Square. Rather than join her mother, Augusta accompanied her brother Richard to Cannes, to find that Sir William had taken a room at the Grand Hotel there. When they later moved to Rome, he followed them. When they went to London, he offered them his London house. A romantic connection, while perhaps not blossoming, was growing steadily.

Augusta eventually returned to Roxborough. Sir William came back to Galway for the fall, then left for London shortly after Christmas. He had lunch with Augusta at Roxborough before leaving, and by the time he reached London, he had made up his mind. He wrote asking Augusta to marry him. Although he was sixty-three and she twenty-eight, he offered her a life of traveling, meeting interesting people, and becoming mistress of all Coole Park had to offer.

The two were married in Dublin at St. Matthias Church on March 4, 1880. Augusta's arrival at Coole Park on July 29 was the occasion for a regional celebration, as she described in her journal: "Left Dublin at 9 a.m. Received at Gort by Canon Daly, Fr.

Shannon and a mob. The Temperance Band played, town decorated, and a triumphal arch with 'Cead Mile Failte' at the gate of Coole."

Coole House: Building the Literary Tradition

In 1768, Sir William's great-grandfather, Robert Gregory, returned to the county of his birth after making his fortune in India and Ceylon. There he purchased a modest estate of six hundred acres. Over time, he added a thousand acres here and five hundred acres there until the estate reached fifteen thousand acres. (Much of it was sold off again in 1857.) He planted fields and forests, constructed and maintained rock walls, and built a large manor alongside Turlough Coole. The house was passed down through the generations of Gregorys. By the time Augusta entered its doors as its mistress, ❷ Coole House was not a working estate but had developed into a house with what a friend called a "fine literary tradition."

Although the spot was and is idyllic, and Lady Gregory appreciated the freedom to explore the library, Coole took some getting used to. She did not feel fully at home until after the birth of her son, Robert:

Yet Roxborough with its romance of river and hillsides came for a long time first in my imagination. It was not until my child's birth that I began to really care for Coole, looking before as well as after. And that love has grown through the long

Coole House, as painted by W. B. Yeats.

years of widowed life, when the woods especially became my occupation and delight.

Perhaps part of the reason she felt the house was cold and lonely in the beginning, especially after the crowded chaos of Roxborough, was that the Gregorys spent much of their time away from it—either at their house in London or abroad—and returned only in the summers.

During the early years of her marriage, when she and Sir William traveled extensively, Lady Gregory's affection for Ireland deepened. She began to pine for her son and, with him, her home. Back at Coole, she explored the surrounding area with greater interest and began other explorations as well—she started to write down her impressions. In addition to her diary, kept sporadically throughout her married life, she wrote a number of sonnets in celebration of her short-lived affair with the English poet Wilfred Scawen Blunt, a few short stories, and a number of articles in support of a variety of political movements.

By the time of her husband's death in 1892, it was a natural progression to step into the task of editing his autobiography, published in 1894. After working on some other writing projects and a visit to the Aran Islands in 1893, Lady Gregory was hungry for more cultural and intellectual stimulation. Her steadfast Anglo-Irish loyalty to both her class and the crown was being chipped away—she was beginning to see in the Irish people a tenacious dignity and the hazy outlines of a rich cultural tradition that had been all but lost.

Up the Avenue of Ilex: The Irish Revival Comes to Coole

Lady Gregory did not need to look too far beyond her own house for kindred souls. From her neighborhood

Yeats described Lady Gregory as "a plainly dressed woman of forty-five, without obvious good looks, except the charm that comes from strength, intelligence and kindness."

and beyond came writers and thinkers whose influence on both her and Ireland was significant. Her most notable visitor was William Butler Yeats, who was visiting her neighbor, the playwright Edward Martyn, at his nearby Gothic castle, Tullira.

Lady Gregory invited Martyn and his guests, including the French critic Arthur Symons, to Coole. When they came a few days later, Lady Gregory asked Yeats what she could best do to direct her efforts toward their common cause of promoting Irish culture. He replied, "If you get our books and watch what we are doing, you will soon find your work."

Each time Yeats was invited back to Coole, he came. And as he frequented Coole, other writers and thinkers

23

came too. Some came with him or to meet with him, while others came just to be at Coole. Visitors included playwright George Bernard Shaw; Yeats's brother, the painter Jack Butler Yeats; writer and aesthete George Moore; agricultural organizer Horace Plunkett; visionary and poet AE; and playwright Sean O'Casey. James Joyce was invited but declined. As noted by John Quinn, a later visitor and Revival supporter, "There seemed to be magic in the air, enchantment in the woods, and the beauty of the place and the best talk and stories I found anywhere."

Of all the visitors to Coole Park, Yeats was perhaps the most frequent and definitely the most pampered. Treated as master of the house, he sat at the head of the table and was given one of the best bedrooms, with nine-foot bay windows looking out on the distant Burren Ridge. It is little wonder that he considered Coole a peaceful retreat from the cares of the world. Lady Gregory had thick, soft carpets laid in the hall outside his room so that he wouldn't be disturbed while working, and she brought cups of beef broth up to him to keep up his strength. He worked when the mood was on him and walked when he could not work.

George Bernard Shaw may have been the most colorful visitor, especially for Lady Gregory's two granddaughters, because Shaw loved to bend the rules. To conserve resources during World War I, Lady Gregory told the girls that they could have either butter or jam on their bread, but not both. One morning at breakfast, they watched Shaw butter his bread, turn it over, and ask for the jam, remarking that he had no butter on his bread. They were shocked that someone could take such liberties with their grandmother's rule and tried to signal her. But Lady Gregory judiciously ignored their gestures, and Shaw went on blithely eating his bread with both butter and jam. Wry humor aside, Shaw was a good guest; he kept the girls captivated with wonderful stories and also played games with them (although he confessed to occasionally cheating).

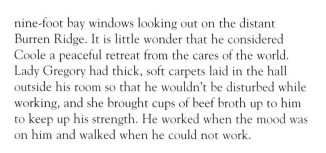

Coole House was a typical landowner's country home, with a wine cellar, library, servant's hall, and gun room, in addition to bedrooms, drawing rooms, and rooms for entertaining.

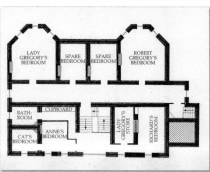

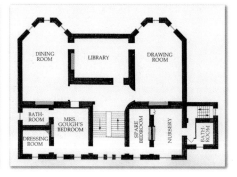

The Burren: A Savage Land

The Burren's name is derived from *boireann*, the Gaelic word for "rocky land." A surveyor for Oliver Cromwell described it as "a savage land, yielding neither water enough to drown a man, nor tree to hang him, nor soil enough to bury." This limestone plateau in northwest County Clare is 216 square miles of exposed rock, grasses and stunted shrubs, and hawthorn trees, dotted with a surprising number of privately owned farms. Springtime brings an explosion of color across the Burren, and summer follows with warmer temperatures on top than in the valley below.

As with many unusual natural landmarks, the Burren plays a part in a number of legends and myths. Most notably, it is said to have the power to bewitch people so that they never leave western Ireland. It certainly worked for Lady Gregory, who contemplated building a house in the Burren area in her later years.

The Burren is one of the most recognizable geographic features in Ireland.

Lady Gregory's special talent was to make her guests feel welcome. Sean O'Casey, who was invited to Coole after his success with *Juno and the Paycock,* immediately felt as at home as Yeats and Shaw did. Writing in his autobiography, *Inishfallen, Fare Thee Well,* Sean O'Casey describes, in third person, his first visit to Coole:

> He hadn't been ten minutes at the table before he felt he had often been there, to eat soberly, and talk merrily of books and theatre, and of the being of Ireland; she in simple in most gracious ways showing how things were handled; pointing out that dese [sic] things were done, not because of any desire for ceremony, but because dey made one more comfortable, and made things easier to eat.

Coole Park was divided on the inside into six half-levels, each reached by a set of central stairs. In the center of the main floor stood the library that had so attracted young Augusta. On one side of the library was the dining room, where literary and cultural conversations raged. On the other side was Lady Gregory's drawing room, where she entertained her guests or, later, sat at her great ormolu table. It had been her husband's writing desk at their house in London; Yeats describes her sitting at it in "Beautiful Lofty Things" (1938).

The Seven Woods: Where Quiet Wanders

Part of Coole's attraction for many visitors lay beyond the comforting, intimate spaces of the house. With Turlough Coole behind the house and the forests planted by Robert Gregory, the grounds offered a plethora of places in which to seek inspiration or just hide away. Lady Gregory planted and nurtured a beautiful walled garden, which remains to this day. Her favorite place was underneath a catalpa tree in one corner of the garden.

One of Yeats's preferred walks while at Coole was in what he called the Seven Woods (in actuality, there are more than seven). He memorializes these woods, as well as the paths leading through them, in a number of poems. He first mentions them in the poetic dedication of his play *The Shadowy Waters* (1906).

Synge also enjoyed these woods, and when he visited Coole, he spent much of his time wandering the paths. Unfortunately, after Lady Gregory's death many of the trees were cut down. They have been allowed to grow back haphazardly, so the forests a visitor sees today are quite unlike what Yeats and his contemporaries walked through.

O'Casey's Scary Seven Woods

Although guests such as Yeats, Synge, and, more recently, the poet Seamus Heaney have found comfort and inspiration in these woods, Sean O'Casey never liked them, describing them as a dark, scary, and barbarous place where Lady Gregory had to do hand-to-hand combat with a thorn bush:

Even wilder than during Yeats's time, the Seven Woods still possess the haunted quality that Sean O'Casey found so striking.

The Seven Woods of Coole with their many winding-paths, so many that it behooved a rambler to go warily that he be not lost in the mazes among the trees. These were among the beloved walks of Yeats, though Sean never cottoned to them, disliking their gloom, with the weight of the gorgeous foliage drooping down, sombre, full of sighs and uneasy rustling, as if God had made them plaintive. Sometimes, what Lady Gregory called a badger cut across their path, and red squirrels shot up the trees at their coming. . . . Here in the Wood of the Nuts, right in their way, callous and impudent, rose a mighty thistle, fully eight feet high, thrusting out its savage barbs towards their breasts, daring them to come on. Then, with the fire of defiance in her eyes, her ladyship charged down on the foe, hissing angrily, one gauntleted hand seizing a spiked branch, while the other stabbed the main butt of the thistle with the chisel-end of the stick, till the branch spikes tottered, bent back, and fell to the ground, a victory celebrated by an uplifted stick and fierce muttering of So perish all de king's enemies!

The Autograph Tree: A Living Guest Book

Among the trees still on the estate is a great copper beech near the north wall of the garden. Carved into the bark of the Autograph Tree are the initials of Yeats, Synge, and many others. As Lady Gregory writes in *Seventy Years*:

And on the great stem, smooth as parchment, of a copper beech whose branches sweep the ground as we come near the gate into the woods, many a friend who stayed here has carved the letters of his name. W.B.Y. of course, and Jack B.Y. with a graving of the little donkey he loves; and J. M. Synge, and AE and An Craoibhin (Douglas Hyde) and John Masefield and Sean O'Casey and as it should be, a very large G.B.S. and this A.J. was cut by Augustus John after his descent from the topmost boughs where he had left those letters also to astonish the birds of the air.

Irish novelist Violet Martin describes the experience of having her name added to the tree:

Today Augusta made me add my initials to a tree already decorated by Douglas Hyde, AE and more of the literary crowd. It was most touching. WBY did the carving, I smoked, and high literary conversation raged and the cigarette went out and I couldn't make the matches light, and he held the little dingy lappets of his coat out and I lighted the match in his bosom. No one was there, and I trust no one saw, as it must have looked very funny.

Although Yeats was one of the first to carve his initials in the tree, O'Casey was one of the most skillful at carving, according to Lady Gregory's granddaughter, Anne Kennedy:

AE's marks on the Autograph Tree.

We actually watched Sean O'Casey carve his name. He was very good at it, and said he had had a lot of practice, as he often carved his name on the door of his tenement flat in Dublin. We were amazed. What an extraordinary thing to do and what on earth was a tenement flat?

It was obviously quite an honor to be included on the tree. Accordingly, Lady Gregory was very specific about whom she wanted to include. Unfortunately, she could not always be around to supervise and was sometimes surprised by the initials she found:

But alas! once or twice country lads doing some work in the orchard, seeing these signatures, thought it natural to add their own, and these unknown to literature, may puzzle some future antiquarian. And once I was just in time to catch hold of the penknives of some schoolboys from the United States who with their friends were spending an afternoon with us. It may be that I was too rash; that some day in that wonder-country there may be signed by a President in the White House the letters of a name that I had disallowed. Have not even angels been entertained unaware?

After Lady Gregory's death and the demolition of the house, so many visitors wanted their initials to share space with those of the honored guests of Coole Park that the Kiltartan Society had to put up an iron fence to prevent further damage.

Turlough Coole: A Disappearing Lake and Nine-and-Fifty Swans

One of Yeats's most-used paths led down to **Turlough Coole,** a seasonal lake that is fed by the Coole River and empties into the ocean via the town of Kinvara.

Because of the peculiarities of the geography, the Coole River, which comes up from a spring in the forest, alternately swells and dries up, and the lake accordingly shrinks and expands. The beautiful setting drew Yeats to its shores, as he describes in his autobiography, *Dramatis Personae:* "I was to know the edges of that lake better than any spot on earth, to know it in all the changes of the seasons, to find there always some new beauty."

Yeats was inspired by this lake to write "The Wild Swans at Coole" (1915), one of his best-loved poems. The first stanza clearly marks the line between Yeats and his subjects: he is on the dry paths; they are on the brimming water. This dichotomy is reinforced when the swans take to the air in the next stanza. He is land-bound, while these "brilliant creatures" are not held

Coole Lake floods and recedes as the seasons change. Sometimes, it even disappears.

back by any ties, as he underscores in the final stanza.

Much has been made of Yeats's anticipation of loss in the poem; he knows that the swans, like strength, beauty, virility, and even poetic power, are transient gifts. Indeed, he alludes to the tremendous changes in Ireland he had witnessed since first coming upon these swans. His declaration that "All's changed since I, hearing at twilight, / the first time on this shore, / The bell-beat of their wings above

Coole House, which hosted many of Ireland's greatest literary and cultural figures, was torn down for the bricks.

my head" is echoed in his poem "Easter Rebellion" (1916). All had changed for Ireland, but Yeats acknowledges in the penultimate stanza that the swans' natural beauty and passion will outlast Irish political change, his own poetic powers, and, perhaps, even the very houses in which he was creating his poetry.

Coole Today:
More Than Just a Moment's Memory

Unfortunately, the Coole estate was indeed caught in the same impermanence. Sir William had bequeathed the estate to his only son, Robert. After Robert's death in the war, the property reverted to his widow, Margaret. Although she grudgingly retained possession of it for

many years, the house was eventually sold to the Ministry of Lands and Agriculture on April 1, 1927. Lady Gregory was allowed to live out the remainder of her days there, paying an annual rent of one hundred pounds.

Nine years after Lady Gregory's death in 1932, the government sold Coole House to a building contractor for the value of the stone. All that is left today is a grassy knoll on top of the foundation, not far from what Yeats imagines in "Coole Park, 1929":

> *Here, traveller, scholar, poet, take your stand*
> *When all those rooms and passages are gone,*
> *When nettles wave upon a shapeless mound*
> *And saplings root among the broken stone*

29

The visitor center at Coole Park hosts exhibitions and seminars.

Sitting on the foundation of the house, looking down on the front steps that now lead into the forest, a visitor can conjure up the spirits of this peaceful place. The woodland paths are still there, the swans still swim on the lake, and Lady Gregory's Autograph Tree still proudly bears the inscriptions of her friends. And although the house no longer stands, a visitor's center offers the opportunity to delve deeper into the literary history.

The center is in one of the original stables, which was renovated to house an exhibition space, an auditorium, and a café. Across the yard are the ruins of the coach house and harness rooms, with the old hand pump still in the center of the yard. In back of the visitor's center is a large, walled-in pasture that used to be the orchards. It is now home to eight red deer, the only species of deer native to Ireland.

Just beyond the visitor's center are the woodland paths that gave Yeats and Synge so much joy. These paths lead through a portion of the thousand acres that now make up the Coole Park–Garryland nature reserve,

which is run by the National Parks and Wildlife Service. The reserve enjoys three separate designations of protection for the landscape, the water, and the wildlife. The woods, especially those north of the garden, are delightfully dark and mystical, ironically more so now than when Yeats walked through them. The trees have been allowed to grow tall, and ivy crawls everywhere. The overhead canopy is thick in the spring and summer, infusing the woods with a green light.

The two major paths through Coole Park are the Family Trail and the Seven Woods Trail. The first is a pleasant walk a little over a mile along well-maintained graveled paths past the visitor's center and deer park to the site of the house and down into the walled garden. Here people gather for lunch at a picnic table, wander across the grass to the Autograph Tree, or sit in the occasional sunshine that creeps out from the clouds. The Seven Woods Trail is a slightly more ambitious trek, past the garden and into the dark Shan-walla and Kyle-na-no woods to the north. The trail loops around to the east through Kyle dortha and Pairc-na-tarav and down to Dim Inchy wood by the lake. After Turlough Coole, the trail returns through Pairc-na-lee to the parking lot.

Kiltartan Cross

Coole Park is now only a fraction of what it once was; in Lady Gregory's day it included vast land holdings. The Gregory clan expanded the estate during the century and a half they owned the land, and they prided themselves on being good landlords to the tenant farmers. Lady Gregory went to great lengths to preserve this impression, declaring in the conclusion of her husband's autobiography, which she edited after

The garden at Coole Park continues to draw visitors to its well-maintained picnic areas and paths.

his death: "I feel it worth boasting that among the first words of sympathy that reached me after his death were messages from the children of the National School at Coole, from the Bishops and priests of the diocese, from the Board of Guardians, the workhouse, the convent, and the townspeople of Gort." Lady Gregory herself became very active in the local community, acting as a mediator in feuds, hosting parties and celebrations, promoting the work of local craftspeople, and establishing a branch of the Gaelic League at the local school that her husband had funded.

Later, Lady Gregory dedicated her translation of *Cuchulain of Muirthemne* (1902) to the people of Kiltartan, the famed area near Coole where the blind poet Raftery met his beloved Mary Hynes: "When I began to gather these stories together, it is of you I was thinking, that you would like to have them and to be reading them." After describing the process of creating the book, she presents the stories as a gift to the people of Kiltartan Cross: "And I am very glad to have something that is worth offering you, for you have been very kind to me ever since I came over to you from Kilchriest, two-and-twenty years ago." She sounds more like an appreciative in-law than a landlord.

Indeed, Lady Gregory and her husband were thankful for and good to the people of the Kiltartan area. One of Sir William Gregory's last acts was to donate money to build a National School. He never lived to see it finished, but he would be proud to see it now. The building served as a National School for years and in

31

The Kiltartan Gregory Museum used to house a school and a branch of the Gaelic League.

1990 was renovated into a museum with the formation of the Kiltartan Gregory Society. The ❸ **Kiltartan Gregory Museum** was opened on August 8, 1996, by Ireland's president, Mary Robinson. Inside is a re-creation of a National School classroom as well as many exhibits covering local history, including the literary heritage of nearby Coole Park, Tullira Castle, Doorus House, and Ballylee.

The Lady Gregory Society

The Lady Gregory Society was formed in 1994 to redress the imbalance of attention paid to the male figures of the Irish Literary Revival and to explore and examine Lady Gregory's literary output. It has been active in preserving and highlighting the literary heritage of the area, hosting an annual Autumn Gathering that includes three days of lectures, presentations, tours, and meetings dedicated to Lady Gregory and her contemporaries. The society also sponsors and facilitates academic work, dramatic productions, and publishing projects.

At the 2005 Lady Gregory Society's Autumn Gathering, Michael Yeats, the poet's son, and Michael Kennedy, great-grandson of Lady Gregory, had time for a rare chat.

Tullira Castle: Fated Meetings

Only a few miles from Coole Park lay ❹ **Tullira Castle,** an enormous Gothic structure with a fifteenth-century tower owned by a friend of Lady Gregory's, Edward Martyn. Martyn was a devout Catholic and ascetic who, although he owned a magnificent castle, slept in a spartan room over the stables. He wrote poetry and a novel and then turned to playwriting.

In August 1896, Martyn invited his friends Yeats and Symons to visit. While there, Yeats attempted to evoke the "lunar power," a mystical force that he believed helped his creativity, by chanting incantations in his room late at night. On the ninth night, he had visions of a centaur and a beautiful naked woman shooting an arrow at a star. Believing that the lunar power had visited him, he told Symons, who said he had also dreamed of a centaur

Edward Martyn hosted Yeats and his friend the critic Arthur Symons at his Gothic castle in 1896.

and a woman, although, tellingly, the woman in his dream was fully clothed.

The other guest in the house, the Count de Basterot (at whose home, Doorus House, Gregory and Yeats would later dream of founding an Irish theater), did not have such a peaceful sleep. He felt such a strong mystical presence that he got up to lock the door in fear. When the highly religious Martyn found out that Yeats had been doing pagan rituals in his house, he was furious and almost kicked him out.

The next day, Martyn's neighbor, Lady Gregory, came to visit and invited the party to Coole for a day. Although Yeats and Lady Gregory had met before, briefly, this time a friendship was cemented. As Symons bitingly noted, Yeats was just what Lady Gregory needed, and she was quick to adopt him: "As soon as her terrible eye fell on him, I knew she would keep him and he would be lost to lyrical poetry." From then on, these two became the nearly inseparable central figures of the Revival and Coole Park became its home.

Given Lady Gregory's increasing interest in the stories and legends of her Gaelic neighbors, and Douglas Hyde's increasing role in bringing both the Irish language and Irish stories to the forefront, it was inevitable that these two would meet, as also happened at Tullira. As Lady Gregory describes it, she was visiting Martyn in 1897 when Hyde arrived, later than expected. Instead of staying on the train until the Gort station, Hyde had gotten off early, in the town of Craughwell, in order to search for folktales among the locals. Enraptured by Hyde's dedication to re-examining Irish culture, Lady Gregory made sure that he accompanied her on her next tour of the surrounding area, near the ancient ruins of Kilmacduagh. She subsequently invited him to Coole Park for a visit, and from then on they scoured the local area together for folktales and Celtic myths.

Hyde had first met Yeats at Trinity College in 1885. The two quickly began trading folklore, with Hyde teaching the tall, awkward poet how to draw stories out of the locals. Hyde was once rhapsodizing about Irish language and culture when a fellow Trinity student asked if he could speak Gaelic. Hyde responded with epigrammatic preciseness, "I dream in Irish."

Doorus House: The Rainy-Day Dream

Just north of Coole Park and Thoor Ballylee, past the charming fishing village of Kinvara, where Lady Gregory set her play *The Rising of the Moon* (1907), is ❺ **Doorus House.** Located at the base of the peninsula between the Galway and Kinvara bays, the house was built by the Count de Basterot in 1866 as a summer home. The front windows offer views across Kinvara Bay to the Burren in the south when the weather is clear. Lady Gregory describes it in *Our Irish Theatre* (1913):

> *The garden was full of flowers. Lavender and carnations grew best, and there were roses also and apple trees, and many plums ripened on the walls. This seemed strange, because outside the sheltered garden there were only stone-strewn fields and rocks and bare rock-built hills in sight, and the bay of Galway, over which fierce storms blow from the Atlantic.*

One of those fierce storms was blowing on an afternoon in 1897 when Martyn and Yeats were visiting de Basterot. The count happened to have another house guest on that wet day—Lady Gregory. She describes that afternoon in her autobiography:

> *And then one day, when E. Martyn and Yeats came to spend a day with the old Count, and rain came on, I had a talk with Yeats as we had tea*

A rainy day at Doorus House on the coast of Galway Bay forced Yeats and Gregory inside, where the conversation turned to the need for Irish plays in Ireland.

together in the steward's office, and the idea came to us that if Maeve could be acted in Dublin instead of London, or Germany, as E.M. had thought of, and with Yeats's Countess Cathleen, it might lead to a theater in which plays by Irish writers might be given in Ireland. It would help to get rid of the stage Irishman, and help to restore dignity to Ireland. This seaside talk was the practical beginning of all that led to the Abbey Theatre, to the dramatic movement.

Buoyed by their initial enthusiasm, the trio retired to Coole Park a few days later and wrote a prospectus to send to everyone they could think of who might be willing to support their endeavors. The letter began:

We propose to have performed in Dublin, in the spring of every year certain Celtic and Irish plays, which whatever be their degree of excellence will be written with a high ambition, and so to build up a Celtic and Irish school of dramatic literature. We hope to find in Ireland an uncorrupted and imaginative audience trained to listen by its passion for oratory, and believe that our desire to bring upon the stage the deeper thoughts and emotions of Ireland will ensure for us a tolerant welcome, and that freedom to experiment which is not found in theatres of England, and without which no new movement in art or literature can succeed.

Raftery

Born in County Mayo on March 30, 1784, Raftery was a blind poet who wandered the Galway countryside reciting poetry and singing songs for his living. As a child he had contracted a horrible case of smallpox that rendered him sightless. His blindness may have had positive effects, however, for he was known to be a poet of extraordinary language and musicality.

According to one popular legend, Raftery would not have traded his poetic ability for sight. As writer Joe Solan tells it, Raftery was walking along the avenue of Killedan House when he heard voices in unison reciting days of the week— "De Luain, De Mairt, De Luain, De Mairt" — continuously. Raftery realized that whoever it was couldn't remember the third day of the week and came to their rescue with "De Ceadaoin"; this obviously broke whatever spell it was that troubled the "good people," for it was their voices he had heard. These "good people" were so grateful that they invited Raftery to a party that lasted for three days, at which Raftery played the fiddle; at the end of this time they asked him for his wish, thinking he would ask for sight, but instead Raftery asked for the gift of poetry.

It was this gift that Raftery brought from town to town, crafting verses either in praise, as in the case of the beautiful Mary Hynes of Ballylee, or in scorn for those who did him wrong. When Raftery died on Christmas Day 1835, he was buried in the Killeeneen graveyard near Craughwell with little fanfare.

Jack Yeats doodled all over this program for the celebration of the poet Raftery. Note the images of W. B. Yeats at top right, Lady Gregory and Jack Yeats at left, and Douglas Hyde at right.

Fifty years later, Lady Gregory began translating Raftery's poems and songs with the help of a tenant farmer named Pat Mulkere. In her search for more Raftery songs and stories, she came across his grave in Killeeneen and worked to give him a proper monument. On August 31, 1902, more than five hundred people, including Lady Gregory, Yeats, Hyde, and Martyn, gathered around the small plot and erected a simple tablet with "Raiferteiri" inscribed on it.

Doorus House commemorates the historic conversation held within its walls with portraits of Martyn, Yeats, Gregory, and de Basterot.

The first letter went out to the poet Aubrey De Vere, who responded generously and positively. Soon to join the list of backers were Maud Gonne, an Irish political activist who had captured Yeats's heart; his Fenian mentor, John O'Leary; the National Library librarian, John Eglinton; and various members of the Irish Parliament.

Doorus House is now a fifty-six-bed youth hostel offering affordable lodgings in a great location. Inside the big sitting room to the right of the front door are portraits of Lady Gregory, Yeats, Martyn, and the Count de Basterot, along with a plaque explaining the house's literary heritage. The area continues to draw thousands of visitors attracted by the peaceful grounds and the wealth of outdoor activities available nearby, from windsurfing and hiking to sunbathing on the beach.

Thoor Ballylee: Yeats's Emblem

In one of Raftery's poems, the stunningly beautiful Mary Hynes brings the poet back to her home at Ballylee, where she offers him food and drink, saying, "Drink Raftery, and a hundred welcomes; there is a strong cellar in Ballylee." It was to this cellar and the tower above it that Yeats came in 1916. He had first seen the tower that he would later name ❻ **Thoor Ballylee** in 1896, when he visited there while staying with Lady Gregory at Coole. As he describes in his essay "Dust Hath Closed Helen's Eye," from the second edition of *The Celtic Twilight* (1902), "There is the old square castle, Ballylee, inhabited by a farmer and his wife, and a cottage where their daughter and their son-in-law live, and a little mill with an old miller, and old ash-trees throwing green shadows upon a little river and great stepping-stones." He had originally come to

Yeats bought Thoor Ballylee as his country home in 1917. The tower became one of his most powerful and personal poetic symbols.

Ballylee to talk with the miller about a legendary healer from County Clare named Biddy Early, who had claimed that "there is a cure for all evil between the two mill-wheels of Ballylee."

Given his sense of peace and contentment while at Coole, it was only a matter of time until Yeats purchased his own place in the area. That opportunity came in 1916 when the Congested Districts Board bought portions of the Coole estate to redistribute among the small landowners of the area. After much negotiation, on March 27, 1917, Yeats was able to buy the tower (which nobody else wanted), the two attached cottages, the walled garden, and the grove of trees across the road for a mere thirty-five pounds. By the end of June, Yeats had taken possession of the tower and was full of plans for renovating it and the cottages.

An Ancient Tower: The Burke Keep

Thoor Ballylee was originally built during the fourteenth century as one of thirty-two fortified residences for the Burke, or de Burgos, family, which ruled over much of that area of Ireland and consequently had to defend themselves against invaders. At the time he bought the tower, Yeats was courting Georgina Hyde-Lees, a young British woman who was the friend of a friend. Although he bought Ballylee and began renovations some months before he married Georgina, it became their summer home during the summer of 1919. Yeats wrote to a friend that Ballylee was "a good house for a child to grow up in—a place full of history and romance, with plenty to do every day."

It needed more work before it could become the refuge Yeats had envisioned, however. He was finally able to return in the spring of 1922 and settle in for the summer season. As he wrote to his friend, Olivia Shakespear, in April, the family was happy to be in Galway, and he had named the castle:

Lady Gregory's son, Robert, painted this dramatic version of Yeats's home.

We are settled here now and our tower much near[er] finishing so that we have a large bed-room with a fine wooden ceiling, but it will be another year, so little labour is there to be got even if our money permitted, before we shall be complete. George is very happy to be back here and declares that the children have at once increased in weight. As I have not seen a paper for days I do not know how far we have plunged into civil war but it will hardly disturb us here. . . . What do you think of our address—Thoor Ballylee? Thoor is Irish for tower and it will keep people from suspecting us of modern gothic and a deer park. I think the harsh sound of "Thoor" amends the softness of the rest.

A few months later, Yeats was soaring to new heights of ecstatic description: "It is a great pleasure to live in a place where George makes at every moment a fourteenth-century picture. And out of doors, with the hawthorn all in blossom all along the river banks, everything is so beautiful that to go elsewhere is to leave beauty behind."

The Poetry of Thoor Ballylee

Ever the poet of place, Yeats did not wait a long time to take the Ballylee of Raftery's poem and make it his. His first poem incorporating Ballylee was a tribute to Lady Gregory's son, Robert, who was killed during a test flight in northern Italy in January 1918. Yeats wrote the poem while staying at Ballinamantane House, which Lady Gregory had lent him while Ballylee was being renovated. In "In Memory of Major Robert Gregory" (1919), Yeats invites the ghosts of his past to dine with him in "in th' ancient tower," to talk until the wee hours, and to "climb up the narrow winding stair to bed." He also mentions Ballylee in "A Prayer on Going into My House" in *The Wild Swans at Coole*.

Because of Ireland's turbulent political situation and Yeats's many literary engagements, he was not able to turn his full attention to Thoor Ballylee as poetic material until he published the collection *The Tower* in 1928. As he describes in a letter written from Ballylee, he needed the calm and private spaces of the country to write poetry:

> *I have all the thought I ever had, but it is a fire of straw. Alas I have to return to Dublin in a couple*

A Troubled Bridge over Water

A central consideration in Yeats's negotiations for the house with the Congested Districts Board was a bridge that ran across the River Cloon and next to the tower. The bridge preserved a right-of-way that led through the property and across the fields. When Yeats agreed to keep the bridge as a right-of-way, the price for the tower came down to something he could pay.

This convenience, however, proved the bridge's demise. During the civil war of 1922, around midnight on August 19, a small band of irregulars blew the bridge skyward. Apparently, the rebel soldiers were incredibly polite. They first knocked on the Yeatses' door and explained what they were going to do; they then gave advice on how best to prevent the windows from getting blown in and made sure everyone was safe. They then blew up the bridge with two huge explosions, thanked the Yeatses, and left.

> *of days. There one gets angry & writes prose but here beside a little stream I write poetry & think of nothing else. I suffer nothing worse than occasional horse-flies which on very hot days drive me on to the castle-roof & into the shadow of the big chimney. I am writing nothing but curses upon old age which distress my wife who says I am not old enough to justify them. I am resisting Wordsworthian calm.*

In the title poem of *The Tower*, Yeats surveys the neighboring lands and thinks about local myths—about Mrs. French, who, in a fit of pique, declared that a local farmer's ears should be cut off, only to have her servant leave and return with that same farmer's ears in a covered dish. He muses on the story of Mary Hynes, whose beauty supposedly drove men mad and compelled one man to drown himself in the bog of Cloone, and the blind poet Raftery, who immortalized Mary Hynes in song. He also thinks back to his own poetic creation, Hanrahan, his alter ego and a symbol of ancient Ireland. In the last section of the poem, Yeats makes out his will, bequeathing "both faith and pride / To young upstanding men / climbing the mountain side." (It may have been for this that Yeats's onetime secretary Ezra Pound called the tower "Ballyphallus.")

Perhaps the best evocation of the tower and its place in Yeats's imagination, though, comes from the "My House" section of the long poem "Meditations in Time of Civil War" (1928):

> *An ancient bridge, and a more ancient tower,*
> *A farmhouse that is sheltered by its wall,*
> *An acre of stony ground,*
> *Where the symbolic rose can break in flower,*
> *Old ragged elms, old thorns innumerable,*
> *The sound of the rain or sound*

Of every wind that blows;
The stilted water-hen
Crossing stream again
Scared by the splashing of a dozen cows;

A winding stair, a chamber arched with stone,
A grey stone fireplace with an open hearth,
A candle and written page.

Much as he does with the shady corners and lake shores of Coole, Yeats creates out of the private spaces of his life enduring public symbols, what he describes in "My House" as "befitting emblems of adversity." He saw in his tower and house representations of his own poetic legacy.

Thoor Today: Yeats's Befitting Emblem

Fortunately, Yeats's tower escaped the fate of Coole House, though just barely. For a variety of reasons, Yeats was unable to return to Thoor Ballylee after 1927, and the house was locked tight. After the death of their parents, Michael and Anne Yeats retained ownership of the property but did little to maintain it. By 1961, the house had returned to much the same state it had been in before Yeats took over. In "Images of a Poet" (1961), D. J. Gordon and Ian Fletcher describe the house:

The ruin has been accomplished with an almost
too dramatic appropriateness; the cottage is now
roofless, the garden overgrown with huge weeds,
the tower roof leaks; graffiti are scribbled on the
wall and window embrasure; rooms have been
stripped of woodwork, and a plank has even been
torn from the great oak door.

Happily, the newly formed Kiltartan Society stepped in to foster interest in the literary history of the district. With funds provided by the Irish Tourist Board, Thoor Ballylee was completely restored. It was reopened as a museum with a speech by the poet Padraic Colum on June 20, 1965.

The museum's walls are adorned with exhibits of Yeats's correspondence, illustrations, and poems. The furniture

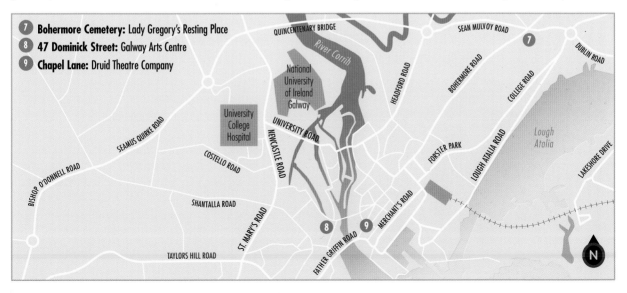

7 **Bohermore Cemetery:** Lady Gregory's Resting Place
8 **47 Dominick Street:** Galway Arts Centre
9 **Chapel Lane:** Druid Theatre Company

is a mix of reclaimed original pieces and reproductions from drawings and photographs. The rooms have been painted in the colors chosen by Georgina Yeats, and the winding stair still leads up to the battlements, where one can look out over the nearby fields and reflect on what gifts to bequeath to the world.

Galway City: Gateway to the Greater World

The closest major city to Coole Park, Thoor Ballylee, and Doorus House is Galway, eighteen miles to the north. Galway, a city of just over seventy thousand, was originally settled by the Vikings but then conquered by Richard de Burgos in the thirteenth century. The de Burgos clan, who ruled over much of Galway, pushed the native Irish across the River Corrib to a rough settlement called the Claddagh. It is from this settlement that the well-known Claddagh ring gets its name.

During the seventeenth century, King William's forces took over the city and forced out the Norman tribes.

According to tradition, if the Claddagh ring is worn with the crown facing in, the wearer is single.

The prosperous and orderly, if not Irish-friendly, city (a decree declared that "neither O nor Mac should strutte or swagger through the streets of Galway") began to go downhill. Lawlessness and disorder gave the town a nightmarish reputation: "Hangings were daily occurrences while reports of seeing the ghosts of noose-bedecked dead men wandering through the streets were nightly events. The banshee was heard wailing, and a ghostly dog called the 'Glumock' reputedly hid in dark corners."

By the late nineteenth century, though, the city had vastly improved and was even beginning to develop its own cultural attractions. Lady Gregory's sister Arabella lived in Galway City, and Lady Gregory often visited her. After Lady Gregory's death in 1932, her body was brought from Coole to Galway's ❼ Bohermore Cemetery (formerly New Cemetery), where she lies alongside her sister.

Galway Today

Contemporary Galway, with the help of European Union and Irish government money, is far more attractive than its seventeenth-century predecessor. Sections of the old town are closed off to cars and are bustling shopping areas. The River Corrib meets the ocean at a pleasant harbor where one can see old-fashioned Galway hookers (wooden sailboats, that is) next to powerboats and fishing trawlers.

One of the many gems Galway offers is the ❽ Galway Arts Centre, 47 Dominick Street. The house is the former Galway residence of the Persse family, and when Lady Gregory came to town, she stayed with her sister, who lived here. The Galway Arts Centre was formed in 1982 to encourage and facilitate all forms of artistic activity. In addition to hosting festivals in literature and the visual arts, the center is home to interesting programs, including the Galway Youth Theatre, which

Quay Street in Galway is a busy pedestrian street popular with both tourists and the many students in town.

collaborated with the Lady Gregory Society on *Through the Coole Door*, a play that weaves together many of the legends Lady Gregory translated along with events from her own life.

Galway is home to another theater company that has earned an international reputation by producing the works of the Irish Literary Revival. Located in Chapel Lane, the ❾ **Druid Theatre Company** was founded in 1975 as Ireland's first professional theater company outside of Dublin. One of its most notable productions was *DruidSynge*, a performance of the entire Synge canon. The show opened during the Galway Arts Festival and, after performances in Dublin and Edinburgh, finished its run on Inis Meáin, the island where Synge spent much of his time while in the Aran Islands.

Chapter 3

The Aran Islands
A Little Corner on the Face of the World

Although they are remote, the Aran Islands have attracted farmers and the attention of writers, including Lady Gregory, W. B. Yeats, J. M. Synge, and Arthur Symons, for centuries.

A cross the mouth of Galway Bay are the last three islands of the European continent. Beyond them is nothing but the North Atlantic. The storms that come in off the ocean batter these islands first, so the inhabitants are of necessity a special breed—a hardy and hardworking people whose independent spirit has attracted scholars and visitors for centuries.

For the creative artists of the Irish Literary Revival, these islands represented a wellspring of Irish culture from which they could collect Gaelic folklore. The Arans also offered a glimpse into a harsher, more basic existence than could be found on the mainland. Irish scholar Ulick O'Connor describes the attraction this way:

> These islands were the last outpost of the culture that was at the root of the literary renaissance. It was almost as if they were acting as a magnet to those who were unconsciously seeking to express the Irish imagination. Here it was concentrated in its purest form in the tales, music, dancing of the people. Their physical appearance, the way they carried themselves, their manner, all suggested the culture they belonged to, so untouched were they by contact with any other.

Whether drawn by the purity of the culture, the dramatic landscape, or the impressive solitude, many of the leading figures of Ireland's Literary Revival came to these rocky islands off the coast of Galway.

Lady Augusta Gregory and the Arans

Of the Revivalist contemporaries, Lady Augusta Gregory was the first to visit the islands. She came on a day trip to the big island of ❶ Inis Mór (also called Aranmor or North Island) on a yacht in 1887. She was beginning to explore the west of Ireland in greater depth and wanted to see firsthand these legendary islands and continue her studies in Gaelic. In her journal, she noted the flannel worn by the children and the "bright shawls" of the women. On a later trip, in 1893, she was marooned for five days on the southernmost island of ❷ Inis Oir (also called Inisheer), taking refuge from a storm in a peasant cottage on the island.

When she returned to the islands a third time, in 1898, she went to Inis Mór with a specific purpose: to collect Gaelic folklore. It was on this trip that she encountered a man who would become an important part of her life and a leading figure in the Revival, the writer John Millington Synge:

> I first saw J. M. Synge in the North Island of
> Aran. I was staying there gathering folk-lore,
> talking to the people, and felt quite angry when I
> passed another outsider walking here and there,
> talking also to the people. I was jealous of not
> being alone on the island among the fishers and
> seaweed gatherers. I did not speak to the stranger,

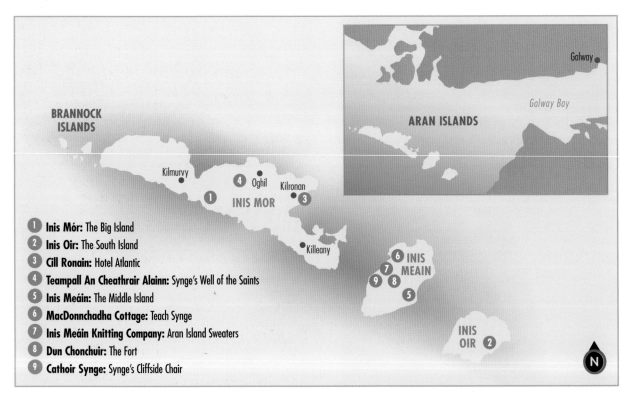

BRANNOCK ISLANDS

ARAN ISLANDS

Galway

Galway Bay

Kilmurvy

❹ Oghil

Kilronan

❶

INIS MOR

❸

Killeany

❻ INIS MEAIN

❼

❾ ❽

❺

INIS OIR ❷

❶ **Inis Mór:** The Big Island
❷ **Inis Oir:** The South Island
❸ **Cill Ronain:** Hotel Atlantic
❹ **Teampall An Cheathrair Alainn:** Synge's Well of the Saints
❺ **Inis Meáin:** The Middle Island
❻ **MacDonnchadha Cottage:** Teach Synge
❼ **Inis Meáin Knitting Company:** Aran Island Sweaters
❽ **Dun Chonchuir:** The Fort
❾ **Cathoir Synge:** Synge's Cliffside Chair

N

nor was he inclined to speak to me; he also looked on me as an intruder, I only heard his name.

Lady Gregory and Synge were not the only literary adventurers to set foot on the Arans. In 1896 William Butler Yeats, Edward Martyn, George Moore, and Arthur Symons came to Inis Mór to look for stories. Their trip was part of the same visit to Galway that brought Yeats and Lady Gregory together for the first time, and Symons wrote about it in the Paris cultural and literary magazine *The Savoy*.

After Yeats's western Ireland tour (which included a swing through County Sligo, where he had spent much of his childhood), he returned to Paris full of enthusiasm for the Aran Islands. He happened to meet Synge at the Hotel Corneille, where Synge had taken a room. As they chatted, Synge shared some of his manuscripts and early attempts at literary and art criticism. Yeats was unimpressed:

> *I said [to Synge]: "Give up Paris. You will never create anything by reading Racine, and Arthur Symons will always be a better critic of French literature. Go to the Aran Islands. Live there as if you were one of the people themselves; express a life that has never found expression." I had just come from Aran, and my imagination was full of those grey islands where men must reap with knives because of the stones.*

> *He went to Aran and became a part of its life, living upon salt fish and eggs, talking Irish for the most part, but listening also to the beautiful English which has grown up in Irish-speaking districts, and takes its vocabulary from the time of Malory and of the translators of the Bible, but its idiom and its vivid metaphor from Irish.*

Synge had grown up in Dublin and County Wicklow and had attended Trinity College, where he excelled in languages. He finished first in his examinations in Hebrew and Gaelic. Pursuing a career in music, he went to Germany to study violin and piano, but after realizing that his shy nature was not suited to giving concerts and recitals, he moved to Paris to become a poet and critic.

Synge headed off to the Aran Islands in May 1898. He spent part of the next five summers on the islands, collecting stories, practicing his Gaelic, and observing the local culture. In addition to his book *The Aran Islands*, material from these experiences fueled a number of his plays, including *The Playboy of the Western World*. As Robert Tracy notes, Synge's time on the Aran Islands deeply affected him and, through him,

J. M. Synge.

greatly altered the public face of Irish drama:

Synge learned in Aran, as Lady Gregory had learned from the Irish-speaking Kiltartan peasants, the idiom that became the vivid and racy dialect of Abbey Theatre comedy, a language based not on Stage Irish, with its begorras and its bedads, but on the daily speech of those who habitually thought in Irish and whose idiom resulted from mentally translating Irish constructions into English.

Synge was able to bring the private language and stories of the island to Dublin and use their vitality to displace the commonly accepted British view of the Irish peasantry. While his portraits of the local characters were not uniformly flattering, the language he put into their mouths breathed with a life and color that had been missing from the public discourse. Synge was able to paint a portrait of a unique people whose dignity and courage had often been overlooked.

Synge often sat or lay atop this cliff, letting the spray from the waves dampen his clothes and paper.

Synge's Aran Islands:
The Little Corner on the Face of the World

As with many of Synge's Revival contemporaries, the poetic energy of his work is inextricably tied to the land. He begins the foreword to *The Aran Islands* with a description of the geography:

> *The geography of the Aran Islands is very simple, yet it may need a word to itself. There are three islands: Aranmor, the north island, about nine miles long; Inishmaan, the middle island, about three miles and a half across, and nearly round in form; and the south island, Inisheer—in Irish, east island—like the middle island but slightly smaller. They lie about thirty miles from Galway, up the centre of the bay, but they are not far from the cliffs of County Clare, on the south, or the corner of Connemara on the north.*

Synge began his Aran Islands trip on the largest island, Inis Mór. He stayed at the ❸ **Hotel Atlantic,** in the main town of **Cill Ronain** (Kilronan), for two weeks while exploring the island and talking with the locals. One of the sites he visited was ❹ **Teampall An Cheathrair Alainn** (Church of the Four Beautiful Saints). The church dates back to the fifteenth century and gets its name from

the four saints said to be buried nearby. For Synge, however, the interesting part was the holy well just south of the church. The water from the well was said to cure blindness and epilepsy. This holy water was the turning point in Synge's play *The Well of the Saints* (1905), in which a priest from Inis Mór restores the sight of two old beggars in County Wicklow.

Dissatisfied with the town of Cill Ronain, which, Synge lamented, "has been so changed by the fishing industry, developed there by the Congested Districts Board, that it has now very little to distinguish it from any fishing village on the west coast of Ireland," he moved on to the least populated and, to this day, least visited of the three islands, ❺ **Inis Meáin** (or Inishmaan): "I have decided to move on to Inishmaan, where Gaelic is more generally used, and the life is perhaps the most primitive that is left in Europe."

Synge based his play *The Well of the Saints* on a legend he'd heard about the Church of the Four Beautiful Saints and a nearby well that was said to cure blindness.

The MacDonnchadha Cottage: Synge's University

Once on Inis Meáin, Synge took up residence in the ❻ MacDonnchadha Cottage (now known as Teach Synge, or Synge's Cottage). Owned by Bríd and Páidín MacDonnchadha, it was a small thatched house in the village of An Cora, and Synge was given the best accommodations, a large room spanning the entire width of the cottage:

> My room is at one end of the cottage, with a boarded floor and ceiling, and two windows opposite each other. Then there is the kitchen with earth floor and open rafters, and two doors opposite each other opening into the open air, but no windows. Beyond it there are two small rooms of half the width of the kitchen with one window apiece.

Synge's mention of the seemingly inconsequential fact that his room had two windows is an example of how he made use of even the smallest details. While he does not dwell on the fact that he had by far the biggest and best room in the cottage, the description hints at both the role of class in his place on the island

The MacDonnchadha Cottage, where Synge stayed during his visits to Inis Meáin. Synge was once locked inside this house for hours when his hosts shut and latched the green door from the outside, completely forgetting the shy and quiet writer was trapped inside.

(Synge came from the Protestant landowner class, as opposed to the Catholic tenant-farmer class of his hosts) and his awareness of how important light and air could be for the islanders:

> Nearly all the cottages are built, like this one, with two doors opposite each other, the more sheltered of which lies open all day to give light to the interior. If the wind is northerly the south door is opened, and the shadow of the door-post moving across the kitchen indicates the hour; as soon, however, as the wind changes to the south the other door is opened, and the people, who never think of putting up a primitive dial, are at a loss.

Given this system of reading the time, a room where one can watch the sun travel across the floor from one window to the opposite is more than just the nicest room in the house; it is a place where one can tell time, can construct the day.

Synge was not the only one to make use of the MacDonnchadha Cottage; others came there to learn Gaelic from the locals. It is claimed that Padraig Pearse and Thomas MacDonagh, leaders of the 1916 Easter Rising, and Lady Gregory stayed there. In fact, so many scholars and Gaelic-language students came that the cottage was called An Ollscoil, which means "the university."

The hub of this "university" was the center room, which served as kitchen, meeting hall, nursery, dining room, and parlor. Synge's description of it upon his arrival is almost lyric in its attention to colors and visual detail:

> The kitchen itself, where I will spend most of my time, is full of beauty and distinction. The red dresses of the women who cluster round the fire on their stools give a glow of almost Eastern richness, and the walls have been toned by the turf-smoke to a soft brown that blends with the grey earth-colour of the floor.

Beyond the Cottage

From the MacDonnchadha Cottage, Synge had an easy walk around the island, which can be covered in a morning. While he walked, Synge often spoke to whoever would exchange words with him. Many times he would walk in the company of a man named Máirtín (Michael in *The Aran Islands*), who served as

Bríd and Páidín MacDonnchadha were Synge's hosts on Inis Meáin.

To move the livestock from tiny pen to tiny pen, farmers must take down the stones and then rebuild the walls after the animals are out.

his guide to the island. Máirtín was the youngest son of Bríd and Páidín, and the two men became friends. They wrote letters to each other, and Synge visited Máirtín when Máirtín moved to Galway for a few years. Máirtín took Synge hunting on the island and answered his questions about how the island worked.

Synge got his best stories from an old man named Pat Dirane. Pat came every day to the MacDonnchadha Cottage to visit with Synge and tell him stories of the island and the fairies he had encountered in his travels. Many of these stories provided the backbone for Synge's plays.

One story from Old Pat was the tale of a cuckolded husband who played dead to catch his unfaithful wife. When she went into the bedroom with a young man, the seemingly dead husband jumped off the table and hit the young man with a stick. This story forms the main plot of Synge's play *In the Shadow of the Glen,* performed by the Irish Literary Theatre in 1903.

The most notable story is one from the oldest man on Inis Meáin, the tale of "a Connaught man who killed his father with the blow of a spade when he was in passion, and then fled to this island and threw himself on the mercy of some of the natives with whom he was said to be related." This story provides the kernel of what was to become Synge's most famous play, *The Playboy of the Western World,* produced at the Abbey Theatre in 1907.

In that play, which Synge set in County Mayo, the young Christy Mahon arrives at a shebeen with a story of how he killed his father with a spade in retribution for a life of misery. The villagers accept him into their community, and he begins to win the heart of Pegeen Mike, the pub owner's daughter. When Mahon's father shows up with a heavily bandaged head, Christy is forced to attack him again. But this time the villagers shy away from the patricide, and Christy is forced to return to his home when his father gets up from the dead a third time.

What is perhaps more remarkable than the original tale, which was also told to Yeats on his visit, is the following observation by Synge:

> *This impulse to protect the criminal is universal in the west. It seems partly due to the association between justice and the hated English jurisdiction, but more directly to the primitive feeling of these people, who are never criminals yet always capable of crime, that a man will not do wrong unless he is under the influence of a passion which is as irresponsible as a storm on the sea. If a man has killed his father, and is already sick and broken with remorse, there can be no reason why he should be dragged away and killed by the law.*

The inhabitants of the bleak Aran Islands had an uneasy relationship with the law. The legal system to them was merely an extension of English rule, and they accorded it little respect. Synge suggests that before the

introduction of the British police to the islands, there was very little crime. When a wrong was done, the perpetrator was given a note to give to the jailer in Galway, and the perpetrator was expected to go serve his time and then return to the island on his own. The islanders believed that loyalty to each other surpassed duty to "the law," especially when that law was carried out by the British constabulary.

This is illustrated by a humorous tale about when the land agents and constabulary came to Inis Meáin to serve evictions for late rents. Synge describes groups of what he calls "mechanical police," in full battle gear, clambering into unstable curraghs to be rowed ashore. During the evictions of very poor islanders who had been unable to pay the rent to their absentee landlords, the policemen rounded up whatever livestock they could confiscate that might bring the landowners a little income. A number of the pigs escaped while being driven to the boats, leaving three policemen lying in the dust. The villagers were ecstatic, as Synge describes: "The satisfaction of the people was immense. They shrieked and hugged each other with delight, and it is likely that they will hand down these animals for generations in the tradition of the island."

In contrast with this humor and gaiety, Synge also describes the eviction of one woman from her home, summarizing the impact on her life in apt terms. The soldiers took the woman outside and proceeded to stack all her furniture outside the cottage home. Then they stacked stones in front of the cottage door to block reentry. Synge realizes that the devastation was more than just material:

> *For these people the outrage to the hearth is the supreme catastrophe. They live here in a world of grey, where there are wild rains and mists every week in the year, and their warm chimney*

corners, filled with children and young girls, grow into consciousness of each family in a way it is not easy to understand in more civilized places.

Synge's gift for keen observation and telling detail brings him close to islanders on the one hand and separates him from them on the other.

Synge is particularly powerful when recording visual impressions and their impact on the psyche. For example, he focuses on the red of the women's clothes, as contrasted against the gray of the surroundings: "No one who has not lived for weeks among these grey clouds and seas can realize the joy with which the eye rests on the red dresses of the women, especially when a number of them are to be found together, as happened early this morning." And, in a passage that is reminiscent of Stephen Dedalus's epiphany at the beach in James Joyce's *A Portrait of the Artist as a Young Man*: "Their red bodices and white tapering legs make them as beautiful as tropical sea-birds, as they stand in a

The Aran Island Sweater

With a constant wind blowing in off the cold Atlantic, and frequent fogs and lashing rains, the Aran Islanders need a thick layer to keep them warm. Many of the men wear traditional Aran Island sweaters, which are made from undyed, cream-colored bainnin sheep wool, black sheep wool, or unwashed wool that retains the waterproofing qualities of the sheep's lanolin. They are usually knit with four to six symmetrical texture patterns, each two to four inches across. The patterns can be complex or simple but usually run from the center of the chest and can run down the arms. Some have designs similar to patterns found in the megaliths on the mainland.

Aran sweaters have been made in the islands for thousands of years, as evidenced by a picture of one in the Book of Kells. Well, that's the story, anyway. Other researchers believe that the sweaters were created around the end of the nineteenth century by a group of enterprising island women looking for additional income. In any case, they gained popularity after Padraig O'Siochain filmed a popular set of documentaries on the islands in the 1950s.

The best place to find these handmade sweaters now is the An Tuirne knitwear shop on Inis Moir. It offers made-to-order heavy wool sweaters in the traditional styles. An even more classic experience can be found at the ❼ Inis Meáin Knitting Company on Inis Meáin. The company's factory, opened more than thirty years ago by Tarlach de Blacam, boasts a dramatic modern showroom looking out on the limestone fields leading down to the water. The shop features knitwear items inspired by the colors of the island and the traditional clothing of the Arans updated for modern lifestyles. Downstairs, the knitwear is packaged and sent to upscale American stores such as Bergdorf's and Saks Fifth Avenue.

These sweaters are made on Inis Meáin based on traditional styles and then shipped around the world.

frame of seaweeds against the brink of the Atlantic." This is a poetry of contrast.

Synge is equally good at painting the details of a landscape that offers little variation: "The slaty limestone has grown black with the water that is dripping on it, and wherever I turn there is the same grey obsession twining and wreathing itself among the narrow fields, and the same wail from the wind that shrieks and whistles in the loose rubble of the walls."

Synge's ability to connect the landscape with the culture led him into the more intimate facets of the islanders' lives. He seemed intensely aware that their sense of being was tied up with the fog and stone in ways he could never fully fathom. Even though he became comfortable on the island, he realized that on some level he would always remain an outsider.

In some ways these men and women seem strangely far away from me. They have the same emotions that I have, and the animals have, yet I cannot talk to them when there is much to say, more than to the dog that whines beside me in a mountain fog.

There is hardly an hour I am with them that I do not feel the shock of some inconceivable idea, and then again the shock of some vague emotion that is familiar to them and.me. On some days I feel this island as a perfect home and resting place; on other days I feel that I am a waif among the people. I can feel more with them than they can feel with me, and while I wander among them, they like me sometimes, and laugh at me sometimes, yet never know what I am doing.

Synge also understood that just as he was struck by the red dresses against the gray of the islands, so too must

he stand out for the islanders. After performing some "simple gymnastic feats and conjurer's tricks" for the people gathered in the schoolmaster's kitchen on a rainy Sunday afternoon, he muses on the legends he has just created: "No doubt these feats will be remembered here for generations. The people have so few images for description that they seize on anything that is remarkable in their visitors and use it afterwards in their talk."

This public role as legend maker was not a natural fit for Synge. He was a private man, happiest when near the action but not part of it. At rehearsals for his plays in Dublin, he sat quietly in the shadows, thoughtfully rolling cigarettes, which he gave to the cast. As Oliver St. John Gogarty noted, Synge rarely seemed to want to be at the center of attention: "He spoke seldom. When he did, the voice came in a short rush, as if he wished to get the talk over as soon as possible."

Dun Chonchuir and Cathoir Synge: The Quiet Places

When Synge needed to withdraw from the islanders to write and think, he found two places that gave him the necessary privacy and solitude. These locations were secluded spaces from which he could observe both the island culture and the natural forces that helped shape that culture.

Near his cottage is a large, fifth-century oval fort on a hill, where Synge would wander to have a smoke after dinner. This ancient fort, ❽ **Dun Chonchuir,** is probably a remnant of an earlier, pagan society and is enclosed by high stone walls, similar to the ring forts on Inis Mór. From within, there is little indication of the outside world. Synge would lie on the twenty-foot-thick walls, smoke, and contemplate these islands and his place on them.

Synge did not go to church with the islanders but often sat watching them as they filed into the tiny chapel on the island. Where they had their church, he had "sea and sky."

Synge's other favorite place, which is not definitively identified in his Aran Islands narrative, is a rough semicircle of stone that he said kept the wind from his back. ❾ Cathoir Synge (Synge's Chair) looks out across Gregory's Sound between Inis Meáin and Inis Mór. It is close to the edge of a cliff leading hundreds of feet down to a tossing sea. The sound of waves that have come from the middle of the Atlantic crashing below one's feet, mixed with the expansive views, can be impressive, as Synge himself describes in this passage, surely written from his seat atop the cliffs:

I have come out to lie on the rocks where I have the black edge of the north island in front of me, Galway Bay, too blue almost to look at, on my right, the Atlantic on my left, a perpendicular cliff under my ankles, and over me innumerable gulls that chase each other in a white cirrus of wings.

The Aran Islands Today: A Legacy Preserved

During the daylight hours, today's Aran Islands would not look much different to Synge. The island is still tightly laced with rock walls. Small terraced fields are still home to goats and cattle seemingly clinging to the sides of the island. Gray skies are still ever-present, and the wind continues to whistle through the rock walls, creating the shrieking that haunted Synge. There is still a sense of being isolated, of being somehow outside of time.

At night, though, the isolation is alleviated because Galway Bay is now almost completely ringed with lights and Galway City, some thirty miles away, brightens the night sky. On a clear night, it is much

Synge would come to Dun Chonchuir, a stone fort near Teach Synge, to smoke, read, and nap.

Another favored place for Synge was Cathoir Synge, a perch on top of a cliff with a pile of rocks to block the wind.

Faster transportation (each island now boasts an airfield as well as an industrial pier), electricity, and access to television and the Internet have begun to transform the culture of these small islands.

harder to ignore County Galway's increasing development. When fog or storms come rolling in, however, and the seas become too rough to navigate, the sense of isolation returns, quickly and definitively.

And although satellite television and the tourist trade have brought in more contact with the outside world, many of the islanders still exhibit the same quiet affinity for solitude that Synge noted. Gaelic is still the language spoken, although many people can also speak English fluently, and certainly without the Irish-English idiom that Synge used in his plays. The people are still a hardworking, tenacious group, adjusting to new developments. They still fish for lobsters with wooden lobster pots, but now their catch is airlifted directly to Paris.

A Literary Landmark in the Making

The islanders on Inis Meáin have not forgotten Synge. During the summer season, his recently renovated cottage is open to visitors who want to see how he lived. His room spanning the width of the cottage is still there, sparsely decorated with an iron bed, a crucifix, and a wooden chair. The owners have re-created the main kitchen and living area, complete with the hearth blackened with turf smoke, woolen socks drying by the fire, a teakettle on the hob, and a table covered with a red-checked cloth. On the table is the one addition, an inviting display of Synge's books as well as articles about the renovation. The public opening of Teach Synge on August 7, 1999, brought such Irish artistic stars as playwright Brian

The Curragh

One of Ireland's paradoxes is the curragh. Given the powerful and often brutal seas around the rocky Aran Islands, it seems reasonable that the men would want the sturdiest, most durable boats they could build. Not so. Curraghs are fifteen-foot boats made from a lightweight wood frame with canvas stretched over it. The canvas is then painted with tar to make it waterproof.

Most curraghs are rowed with two oars on either side, and some run a rudimentary sail up in the front. These extremely lightweight and responsive boats float high in the water, reducing the likelihood of getting swamped by high seas. Because the hull of the boat is simply stretched canvas, the men don't wear regular shoes or boots in their boats; instead, they wear pampooties (lightweight shoes made of leather).

Synge, who had numerous shaky but successful trips in curraghs, found the experience thrilling: "I enjoyed the passage. Down in this shallow trough of canvas that bent and trembled with the motion of the men, I had a far more intimate feeling of the glory and power of the waves than I have ever known in a steamer."

These fragile wooden and canvas boats provide quite a ride in the rough Atlantic waters around the Arans.

Inside the newly renovated Teach Synge, the hearth looks as it did in Synge's day.

Friel and actor Stephen Rea, as well as some three hundred others, to Inis Meáin in celebration of Synge's legacy.

Nor is the local population unfamiliar with Synge's writings. When the Druid Theatre Company put together its *DruidSynge* production, the company came to Inis Meáin to perform in the location where Synge gathered so much of his material, just as a Japanese company stayed on the island for weeks before beginning its production of *Playboy*. Actors, directors, producers, and writers regularly come to the island to get a feel for Synge's work and to talk to

islanders about their perspectives. In addition, Synge's legacy has found expression in the work of Martin McDonagh, whose plays, including *The Cripple of Inishmaan* and *The Lieutenant of Inishmore*, have been successfully produced at the Abbey Theatre in Dublin and abroad.

As this chapter begins with Synge's description of geography, so it ends with his reflection on the people of Aran: "I became indescribably mournful, for I felt that this little corner on the face of the world, and the people who live in it, have a peace and dignity from which we are shut for ever."

Chapter 4

County Mayo
A Queer Lot These Times

The often-surreal landscape of County Mayo inspired the stories of George Moore as well as the fantastic plot of J. M. Synge's *The Playboy of the Western World*.

County Mayo sprawls over two thousand square miles and is the third largest county in Ireland. It can be bleak and desolate, yet starkly striking. In addition to a rocky, jagged coastline, it features mountains in the north, fields in the eastern section, and the country's largest bog.

This area of nearly 120,000 people played a significant role in the Irish Literary Revival. Playwright and novelist George Augustus Moore was born here in 1852 to a wealthy Catholic landowner; he spent many of his formative years in the county before moving abroad to pursue a writing career. He later portrayed the oppressed people of County Mayo in his collection of short stories, *The Untilled Field*. The area's striking landscapes also inspired two of the Revival's popular plays: *Cathleen Ni Houlihan*, by Lady Augusta Gregory and William Butler Yeats, and *The Playboy of the Western World*, which is set in Mayo, by John Millington Synge.

Moore Hall: The Tilled Field

Set in the middle of a triangle marked by the towns of Castlebar, Claremorris, and Ballinrobe was an estate of more than twelve thousand acres along Lough Carra. The big three-story house called ❶ Moore Hall, built in 1795, was a fully self-contained estate with farm stables, gardens, a mill, a brewery, and a cooperage that employed many of the locals. Its first owner was George Moore, who, after making a fortune in the wine and brandy trade out of

Spain, returned to the county of his ancestors and built the house. In addition to being a kind and caring landlord, Moore was unusual for another reason: he was part of a small group of Catholic landlord gentry.

The house passed to his son, George Henry Moore, during the middle of the nineteenth century. The estate was especially notable for the fact that no evictions were ever recorded in the Moore demesne, and, even more impressively, nobody died of starvation on the Moore estate during the famine years. That is amazing given that nearly a third of the population of the county perished during that time. George Henry

Moore became the member of Parliament for the county in 1847 and helped found the Irish Independent Party. He was so beloved in the area that when he died, his coffin was carried by sixteen of his tenants and attended by farmers from throughout the county.

By the time George Henry Moore's son, George Augustus Moore, reached his twenties, he had left Ireland and settled in Paris with the intent of becoming a painter. Although that didn't pan out, he certainly had wonderful taste in friends, getting to know Degas, Manet, and Renoir. Another friend was novelist Emile Zola, who encouraged him to become a writer. In 1880,

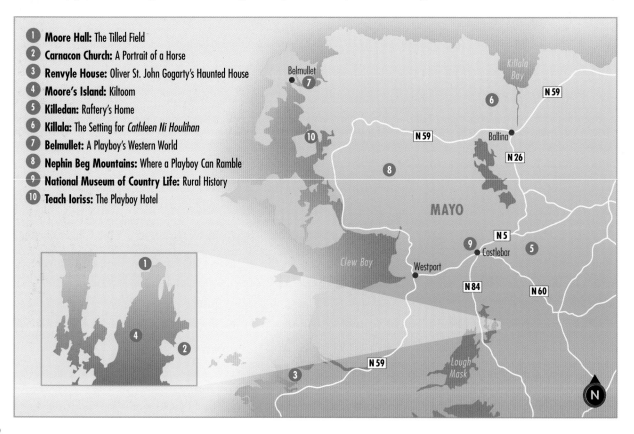

1. **Moore Hall:** The Tilled Field
2. **Carnacon Church:** A Portrait of a Horse
3. **Renvyle House:** Oliver St. John Gogarty's Haunted House
4. **Moore's Island:** Kiltoom
5. **Killedan:** Raftery's Home
6. **Killala:** The Setting for *Cathleen Ni Houlihan*
7. **Belmullet:** A Playboy's Western World
8. **Nephin Beg Mountains:** Where a Playboy Can Ramble
9. **National Museum of Country Life:** Rural History
10. **Teach Ioriss:** The Playboy Hotel

Although George Moore described Moore Hall as standing "on a pleasant green hill, with woods following the winding lake," he found the locals to be melancholy and awkward. He portrayed a man he met while biking with AE as being similar to the ones he would see at Moore Hall: "ratlike faces with the long upper lip that used to come from the mountains to Moore Hall, with banknotes in their tall hats, a little decaying race in knee-breeches, worsted stockings, and heavy shoon, whom our wont was to despise because they could not speak English."

The Horse of Dreams

In 1846, when things were at their bleakest during the Great Famine, George Henry Moore did what many of his fellow landlords might have done; he went to the horse races. He had more than just entertainment on his mind, however. Bringing his horse across Ireland by train and to England on the overnight ferry, George Moore entered Coranna in the 1846 Chester Gold Cup with long odds to win. The horse pulled away and crossed the finish line first, netting Moore seventeen thousand pounds. He used the money to buy English grain and cows to give to his tenants. A portrait of Coranna now hangs in the ❷ **Carnacon Church,** near the Moore estate.

When Coranna won a race in England, the tenant farmers of the Moore estate reaped the benefits; this portrait hangs in Carnacon Church.

Manet's painting evoked scorn among Moore's Paris friends, and this portrait was renamed *Le noyé repêché* (*The Drowned Man Fished Out*). In his defense, Manet protested, "Is it my fault if Moore has the look of a broken egg yolk . . . or if the sides of his face are not aligned?"

Moore moved to London, though he still spent much time in Paris.

It was in part his involvement with the Irish Literary Theatre that brought Moore back to live in Ireland in 1901. He had helped with the London rehearsals of *The Countess Cathleen* and *The Heather Field* during the theater's first season in the spring of 1899. He spent that fall rewriting his cousin Edward Martyn's play *The Tale of a Town* as *The Bending of the Bough,* which was produced in 1900. Moore collaborated with Yeats on a play called *Diarmuid and Grania,* which went onstage in 1901. When their next joint venture went awry, Moore left the Irish Literary Theatre in disgust. He tried to get a traveling company of Gaelic actors to present plays across the more remote areas of Ireland, but that idea lost momentum when priests in the Gaelic League moved to suppress the project.

Moore was having even less luck taking a leadership role in the Gaelic League. The combination of having written an earlier book that was critical of Ireland, his inability to speak Gaelic, and the fact that he was now, in spite of his Catholic upbringing, staunchly anti-Catholic made his advancement prospects in that organization slim at best. A friend of Moore's, Father Tom Finlay, suggested that he write fiction that could be translated into Irish and provide models for young Irish writers to follow. Once he had decided on a format, a series of interrelated stories as in Turgenev's *A Sportsman's Sketches*, Moore did not have to travel far to find subjects.

Around County Mayo: A Return to the Fields

In conjunction with his growing involvement in the Irish Literary Revival, Moore began to spend more time at the family house on the shores of Lough Carra. It was here, among the rural and sometimes bleak country roads and remote villages of County Mayo, that Moore found a way to contribute to the Revival. As Richard Allen Cave notes in his introduction to *The Untilled Field*,

> *Moore's preoccupation in the stories that make up* The Untilled Field *with revealing to the alert, sensitive reader the inner wealth of individuals who might on first acquaintance appear to lead grey, quiet lives was wholly in accord with the aims of the cultural renaissance at large, which sought in every branch of the arts to redeem the presentation of Irish characters from British modes of perception which tended to reduce them to type-figures at best and at worst to caricatures. Moore brought dignity and emotional complexity to the study of Irish rural life even as Joyce subsequently was to bring them to the study of the Dublin poor.*

Silly Government Programs

In 1890, the chief secretary of Ireland for the English government formed what was called the Congested Districts Board, with the purpose of developing agriculture and industry in the poorest areas of Ireland. The board's influence and jurisdiction spread from Donegal in the north all the way south to County Cork. Funded by grants from the English government, the board attempted many projects to help the poor of western Ireland. Some of their projects and policies had positive benefits, while others did little good or were just a waste of money. For example, the board employed men in creating roads that led nowhere just to get them working. In Moore's story "A Playhouse in the Waste-Land," in *The Untilled Field*, Father James describes the board's work:

Men working on projects sponsored by the Congested Districts Board built roads like this one, sometimes leading to nowhere.

> "The policy of the Government," he said, "from the first was that relief works should benefit nobody except the workers, and it is sometimes very difficult to think out a project for work that will be perfectly useless. Arches have been built on the top of hills, and roads that lead nowhere. A strange sight to the stranger a road must be that stops suddenly in the middle of a bog. One wonders at first how a Government could be so foolish, but when one thinks of it, it is easy to understand that the Government doesn't wish to spend money on works that will benefit a class. But the road that leads nowhere is difficult to make, even though starving men are employed upon it; for a man to work well there must be an end in view, and I can tell you it is difficult to bring even starving men to engage on a road that leads nowhere."

It is this fine balance of a critical, analytical eye and a sympathetic heart that Moore achieves in this collection. His greatest accomplishment is that he wrote about the lives of his tenants without sinking into the patronizing tone that marked his earlier book, *Parnell and His Island*: "*The Untilled Field* sets out to render the quality of peasant and urban working-class life, to evoke what it is in Ireland to be poor and near-destitute in terms of material well-being."

In the beginning, though, Moore's goal for the project was slightly less ambitious. In the preface to the 1926 edition, Moore places the book within the context of the Irish Literary Revival:

> *We all did something, but none did what he set out to do. Yeats founded a realistic theatre, Edward emptied two churches he and Palestrina between*

them and I wrote *The Untilled Field, a book written in the beginning out of no desire of self-expression, but in the hope of furnishing the young Irish of the future with models.*

Models from the Earth

Once he began, Moore found inspiration everywhere he looked in Mayo: "Story followed story, each coming into my mind before the story on the blotting pad was finished, and each suggested by something seen or something heard." The models Moore presents in *The Untilled Field* are complex characters accurately sketched without flourish or stylistic clutter. His men have trouble seeing their way clear to the right path, and his women struggle with the weaknesses and mean streaks that affect us all. His characters deal with incompetence, lost dreams, and cross-purposes. In the leading story, "The Exile," Catherine, James's beloved, reveals that she is really in love with James's brother Peter, farmer Pat Phelan's impractical son with no head for farming. That the story ends with James leaving for America and the untalented Peter set to take over the farm with his new wife illustrates that, for the poor people of Mayo, there are no easy solutions.

Whether he is describing the desperate schemes of a priest riding his bicycle through the bogs of Mayo and building a playhouse for a play that will never be produced, or telling of a mystic woman who sees visions in the stained glass she paid to put in her local church, Moore tries to sketch "grey, quiet lives" into a picture greater than themselves. He wanted to "paint the portrait of [his] country and this could only be done in a Catholic atmosphere."

This panorama in turn, he believed, inspired one of the greatest works to come out of the Revival. Musing on where J. M. Synge got his inspiration for *The Playboy of the Western World*, Moore suggests that his own book

Four Removes from Reality: Playwriting with Yeats and Moore

When the abstract and poetic Yeats worked with the realist novelist George Moore on the dramatic retelling of an ancient Irish myth (*Diarmuid and Grania*), there was bound to be some working at cross-purposes. Yeats wanted to write the play in Galway dialect; Moore felt that only the language of the Bible would do. They argued in circles.

One night, Yeats burst into Moore's room with the solution: write the play in French! Yeats proposed, "Lady Gregory will translate your text into English, Taidgh O'Donoghue will translate the English into Irish, and Lady Gregory will translate the Irish text back into English." So after the play was conceived and outlined in English, written in French, translated into English, translated into Irish, and translated back into English, Yeats added the finishing touches to the style. It's amazing that the play was performed at all.

Where once Moore Hall resounded with the literary banter of AE, Lady Gregory, Edward Martyn, Douglas Hyde, and William Butler Yeats, now there is only silence and the occasional whisper of the wind in the trees.

was responsible: "It seemed to me that I had come upon the source of Synge's inspiration. *The Untilled Field* was a landmark in Anglo-Irish literature, a new departure, and Synge could not have passed it by without looking into it."

Moore Hall in Ruin

In time, the house that had been continuously occupied for more than a hundred years became a victim of family dynamics and local politics. Moore had a

Haunted Ireland

There may be another set of occupants of Moore Hall—supernatural ones. Some visitors claim to have heard footsteps inside the house, doors slamming, and loud animated talking or a child's laughter. The massive, crumbling edifice is certainly the right atmosphere for ghosts, as commentator Richard Jones notes: "It is a gaunt shell of broken walls, toppled brick and fallen masonry. The gnarled branches of skeletal trees poke from empty windows, whilst its basement is a sinister labyrinth of arched corridors and dark rooms, their floors carpeted by a mulch of decaying leaves and squelching mud."

Moore Hall is only one of many ruined houses that dot the Mayo countryside.

In a country with so many abandoned houses and tragic stories, Moore Hall is not the only place boasting tales of hauntings and supernatural occurrences. There are hosts of books and websites on the subject. Yeats was obsessed with the supernatural and spent much of his time on mystical projects. Numerous tales exist of Yeats attempting to contact dead spirits through automatic writing or séances.

For example, at ❸ **Renvyle House,** the Connemara home of Dublin surgeon and poet Oliver St. John Gogarty, Yeats and his wife encountered the ghost of a "red-haired, pale-faced boy" and learned that he was the son of the house's former owners. Yeats also claimed to have contacted the spirits of Synge and Lady Gregory at séances in America. At a séance in Dublin when he was young, Yeats was gripped by evil spirits and began banging his head on the table, according to

his friend Katherine Tynan. As Yeats relates in *Reveries*, he was forced to rely on literature to save himself:

> *I was now struggling vainly with this force which compelled me to movements I had not willed, and my movements became so violent that the table was broken. I tried to pray, and because I could not remember a prayer, repeated in a loud voice—*
>
> *"Of Man's first disobedience and the fruit*
> *Of that forbidden tree whose mortal taste*
> *Brought death into the world, and all our woe . . .*
> *Sing, Heavenly Muse."*

Apparently, these opening lines of Milton's *Paradise Lost* worked, because the room became still and the troubling spirits departed.

falling-out with the other members of the Literary Revival over Yeats's and Lady Gregory's obsession with folk drama. After his subsequent return to London, the doors of Moore Hall were opened only sporadically. Following the December 6, 1921, Anglo-Irish treaty that granted most of Ireland its independence (the six northern counties retained their British status), anti-treaty militias targeted Moore's brother Maurice, who was actively supporting the freshly minted Irish Republic. In January 1923, the antitreaty militias burned Moore House, leaving only the brick, iron, and Italian plasterwork that are there now.

With no heirs, George eventually sold much of the property to the Irish Land Commission. The land has now passed into the control of a lumber company that manages the forests. There have been discussions about restoring Moore Hall, but it remains an empty shell surrounded by spruce, pine, and ash trees.

A few hundred yards up a grassy path overhung with branches, a visitor catches a glimpse of the huge stone house through the trees. Looking like a movie set in the middle of the woods, the remains of Moore Hall are still impressive—it is easy to imagine the symbol of power and tradition this house used to be. Yeats, AE, Lady Gregory, and Edward Martyn all visited here, reveling in literary conversation and the natural beauty of the grounds. Now it is home to birds, animals, and the occasional late-night teenagers' party.

When Moore died, his body was brought from his home in London to the estate his father and grandfather had so carefully maintained. He was brought back not to the house, which by then had been a burned-out shell for ten years, but to Castle Island in the nearby lake, Lough Carra. The island, which is known locally as ❹ **Moore's Island,** has a family plot where Moore's ashes are buried near the remains of his ancestors. It is a fifteen-minute boat ride from the shore in front of Moore Hall, and the grave has a monument with a plaque in memory of the Moores buried there. Moore's close friend the mystic poet AE wrote the epitaph, which reads, "He forsook family and friends for his art; but because he was faithful to his art his family and friends reclaimed his ashes for Ireland."

W. B. and Georgie Yeats stayed at Renvyle House, now a hotel, on their honeymoon in 1917.

George Moore's headstone.

On a Wild Coast: A Playboy's Home

Moore was not the only writer struck by the bleak and dramatic coast of this part of western Ireland. A number of small towns in the region figure in the lives and works of Revival writers.

The itinerant poet Raftery wrote about his beloved home of ❺ **Killedan,** "Killedan the village where everything grows, / There are blackberries there and all that is good, / And if I were standing in the midst of my people, / Age would leave me and I'd be young once more."

Yeats and Lady Gregory set their nationalist drama *Cathleen Ni Houlihan* in the small town of ❻ **Killala,** overlooking Killala Bay, on the northern coastline of Mayo near the Sligo border. It was here in August 1798 that General Humbert landed his French forces to aid an Irish uprising against the British. After taking the city, the forces settled in the bishop's residence, only to be driven out later as the uprising failed.

On a bicycle tour of Mayo in 1904, J. M. Synge found in the remote area near the town of ❼ **Belmullet** the setting he needed to flesh out an anecdote he'd heard on the Aran Islands. The tale was about a man who had killed his father and run off to Inis Meáin, where he was hidden by the islanders until he could

escape to the United States. Here is how Synge describes the story in *The Aran Islands:*

> He often tells me about a Connaught man who killed his father with the blow of a spade when he was in passion, and then fled to this island and threw himself on the mercy of some of the natives with whom he was said to be related. They hid him in a hole—which the old man has shown me—and kept him safe for weeks, though the police came and searched for him, and he could hear their boots grinding on the stones above his head. In spite of a reward which was offered, the island was incorruptible, and after much trouble the man was safely shipped to America.

That story, the same story that Yeats heard on Inis Mór when he visited with Symons in 1896, was the

The market in Belmullet, c. 1900.

Christy dreams of running away to the Nephin Beg Mountains with Pegeen Mike in *The Playboy of the Western World*.

foundation of *The Playboy of the Western World*—the play that incited riots, got its cast arrested, and gave Synge his lasting reputation.

The play—which can be read as a comedy or a drama, for it has elements of both—examines what happens when a young man named Christy Mahon arrives in a lonely wayside pub with a story about having killed his father. Instead of reacting with horror and fear, the locals are impressed. The publican hires Christy to work in the pub alongside his daughter, Pegeen Mike, who happens to be affianced to the insecure and easily frightened Shawn Keogh. Pegeen Mike's affections are soon turned toward the heroic Christy, who, in

In Synge's *The Playboy of the Western World,* Christy Mahon escapes to this desolate coast after splitting his father's skull with a shovel . . . or so he thinks.

addition to having parricide on his conscience, has poetry on his tongue and the vitality to beat all the locals in the games on festival day.

While the play's basic premise, a man being welcomed into a community for killing his own father, may come off as a bit of a stretch, Synge had good reason for believing that it would ring true. After all, it was based on a story both he and Yeats had heard, and the old man who had told it to him had explained why the islanders had hidden the criminal. In addition, some critics have pointed to another anecdote Synge had heard about a Mayo man who had assaulted a woman and then escaped the police with the help of his "woman friends," who were charmed by him.

In any case, the village "on a wild coast of Mayo" (as Synge writes in the setting note to the play) is the type of place where the strange is commonplace. As Pegeen Mike explains to her fiancé, their world is full of people such as "Red Linhan, has a squint in his eye, and Patcheen is lame in his heel, or the Mad Mulrannies were driven from California and they lost in their wits. We're a queer lot these times to troubling the Holy Father on his sacred seat." The local population in the play is drunk, on its way to getting drunk, nervous, spineless, or deformed in some way. The local heroes, or at least people who have done deeds worth noticing, are the criminals: "Daneen Sullivan [who] knocked the eye from a peeler [a policeman], or Marcus Quin, God rest him, got six months for maiming eyes."

If this land is a strange and occasionally dangerous one full of "harvest boys with their tongues red for drink" and "the thousand militia . . . walking idle through the land," it also offers nature as a refuge for lovers. One example is Christy's poetic description of what he and Pegeen Mike can do in the nearby ❽ **Nephin Beg Mountains:** "Then yourself and me should be pacing Neifin in the dews of night the times sweet smells do be rising, and you'd see a little shiny new moon, maybe, sinking on the hills." In Christy's idyllic vision of the future, his nights would be spent out among the hills before returning to Pegeen: "Isn't there the light of seven heavens in your heart alone, the way you'll be an angel's lamp to me from this out, and I abroad in the darkness, spearing salmons in the Owen, or the Carrowmore."

Mayo Today

With plans to rebuild Moore Hall and hotels boasting of their connection to Synge, Mayo is aware of its rich cultural and literary heritage. One of the major attractions is the ❾ **National Museum of Country Life** in Castlebar, near Moore Hall. This multimedia facility has exhibits illustrating the traditions and daily life of nineteenth- and twentieth-century rural Ireland. For Synge fans, ❿ **Teach Ioriss,** a modern hotel built on the site of the inn where Synge stayed while gathering material for *Playboy,* is another important stop on a literary pilgrimage to Mayo.

The main attraction in the area, however, continues to be the dramatic landscape and outdoor activities. Many of the beaches, including those at Blacksod and Broadhaven Bays, where Christy performs his athletic feats, are well-known fishing spots, as are many of the rivers in the area, including the Owenmore and the River Deel. For the hiker, the Nephin Beg Mountains, where Christy wants to take Pegeen for moonlight strolls, offer a wide variety of hiking options. The range is a series of fourteen peaks, the highest of which is Nephin Beg, at slightly more than two thousand feet. And just north of these mountains lie the seaport and county that helped inspire even more poetry—Sligo.

Chapter 5
Sligo
The Land of Heart's Desire

Yeats often came to Glencar Lake, beneath the ridge of Ben Bulben, to hunt for fairies and magical creatures.

Although W. B. Yeats was born in Dublin, spent much of his childhood in London, enjoyed his summers at Coole Park, and bought a tower house in Ballylee, he was in many ways a poet of Sligo. His mother's family was from Sligo, and it was to here that he was shipped for summers during his childhood. As he writes in *Reveries over Childhood and Youth* (1916), his time in Sligo had a tremendous impact on him: "Years afterwards, when I was ten or twelve years old and in London, I would remember Sligo with tears, and when I began to write, it was there I hoped to find my audience." He claimed that he continued to visit the woods in Sligo around Dooney Rock and Ben Bulben at night in his dreams long after he'd left the county for good.

The time spent with his grandfather and uncle, his interactions with the local Catholic and Gaelic neighbors, and his friendships with the beautiful Gore-Booth sisters of Lissadell House all influenced his intellectual development, but the sheer beauty and mystical appeal of the land had the greatest effect on Yeats. Many of his most famous and successful poems are set in the countryside around Sligo or deal with stories he heard from natives of the county— poems that speak of waterfalls and islands, of Queen Maeve riding out from a hidden door in a mountain, of secret woods, and of a lakeside fiddler whose songs are so sweet they guarantee his place in heaven. "Drumcliff and Rosses were, are, and ever shall be, please Heaven! places of unearthly resort. I have lived near them and in them, time after time, and have gathered thus many a crumb of faery lore."

Yeats's poems sing the praises of a county of seven hundred square miles of grassy hills overlooking sandy beaches, wide farmlands, soaring limestone cliffs, and picturesque mountain lakes. With the port of Sligo set in the middle, County Sligo ranges out on both sides and flattens to the east with Lough Gill, which it shares with County Leitrim. Sligo Town is a rough, bustling city of sixty thousand people in the process of remaking itself with the help of European Union money.

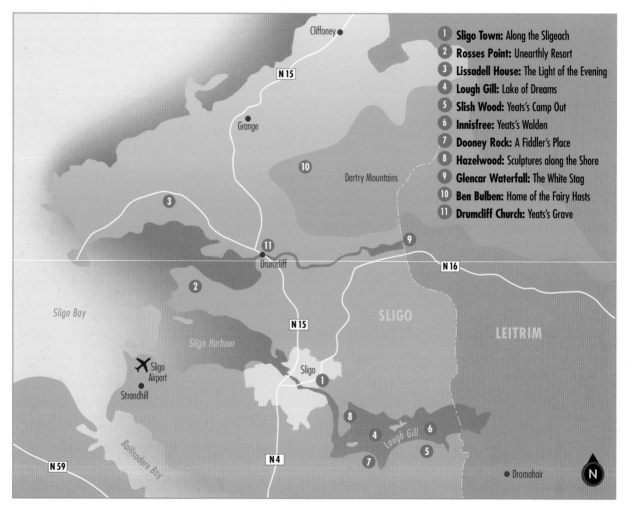

1. **Sligo Town:** Along the Sligeach
2. **Rosses Point:** Unearthly Resort
3. **Lissadell House:** The Light of the Evening
4. **Lough Gill:** Lake of Dreams
5. **Slish Wood:** Yeats's Camp Out
6. **Innisfree:** Yeats's Walden
7. **Dooney Rock:** A Fiddler's Place
8. **Hazelwood:** Sculptures along the Shore
9. **Glencar Waterfall:** The White Stag
10. **Ben Bulben:** Home of the Fairy Hosts
11. **Drumcliff Church:** Yeats's Grave

Sligo Town

❶ **Sligo Town** lies at the mouth of the River Garavogue and at the end of Sligo Bay. The town name comes from the Gaelic *sligeach*, meaning "place of shells." Indeed, the soil contains oyster, cockle, mussel, and limpet shells, along with traces of settlements going back as far as 3000 B.C. The main town dates its modern history to the ninth century, when it was an important gateway village and, as such, was sacked by the Vikings. It was later fortified, but few of those medieval ramparts have survived. The town lies along the River Garavogue, from the Rockwood Parade to the Douglas Hyde Bridge at St. Stephen Street.

Rosses Point

Just north of Sligo is the small fishing resort of ❷ **Rosses Point,** where Yeats visited a cousin of his and, later, his uncle, George Pollexfen. Rosses Point is a typical summer resort community, ranged out along the shore of Drumcliff Bay, looking out over the harbor to the mountain of Knocknarea. Yeats visited his uncle "sometimes because I could not afford my Dublin lodging, but most often for freedom and peace."

Primarily, "freedom and peace" meant that Yeats could walk the hillsides and secret paths looking for ways to express his feelings about the landscape in his poetry. He even recruited help at times from his Sligo family.

During Yeats's childhood, Sligo was a bustling seaport.

Wanting to hear the sounds of the sea birds that start flying before dawn, Yeats once woke his reluctant cousin and insisted that they go out on the water. They sailed out of the harbor, but the wind died and they were stuck. Yeats rolled up in the mainsail and went to sleep. The cousin woke him for money to buy fish so they could at least pretend they were successful fishermen, but Yeats had no money, so they returned home empty-handed. But the dawn sea birds were imprinted on Yeats's imagination; they resurfaced in *The Shadowy Waters* (1906), where they haunt the play:

Dectora: What is there but the crying of the birds?
Forgael: If you'll but listen closely to that crying
*   You'll hear them calling out to one another*
*   With human voices. . . .*
*   They're crying out, could you but hear their words,*
*   "There is a country at the end of the world*
*   Where no child's born but to outlive the moon."*

It was here and at the nearby town of Ballisodare that Yeats had some of his earliest encounters with the

Yeats described Rosses Point as "a little sea-dividing, sandy plain, covered with short grass like a green tablecloth, and lying in the foam midway between the round cairn-headed Knocknarea and 'Ben Bulben, famous for Hawks.' "

supernatural and the occult, which would become one of his many obsessions. At his cousin's house, he heard spirits thumping walls and walking though the house. Outside, he saw lights like torches suspended above the river and moving quickly up the sides of nearby Knocknarea. Later, in Rosses Point, Yeats saw a fire blaze up near him late in the night and another fire spark up seemingly in answer from the slopes of Knocknarea. He describes this area in *The Celtic Twilight* as "chokeful of ghosts. By bog, road, rath, hillside, sea-border they gather in all shapes: headless women, men in armour, shadow hares, fire-tongued hounds, whistling seals, and so on." He began advising people to "believe whatever had been believed in all countries and periods."

Jack Yeats and *Memory Harbour*

W. B. Yeats was not the only Yeats sibling to have a close connection to Sligo and Rosses Point. His younger brother Jack spent even more time in the west of Ireland. Born in 1871, six years after WBY, Jack attended art school in England before returning to live in Ireland in 1910. He made periodic visits to his relatives in Sligo and was welcomed at Gregory's Coole Park, where a number of his paintings hung on the walls. He also made a tour of Connemara and Mayo in 1905 with J. M. Synge, who was reporting on the conditions of the peasants for the *Manchester Guardian* while Jack made a series of sketches to accompany the stories.

Jack Yeats is now recognized as one of Ireland's most important twentieth-century artists, with works in the Hugh Lane Gallery, the National Gallery, and the Tate.

Yeats wrote about this painting: "When I look at my brother's picture, *Memory Harbour*—houses and anchored ship and distant lighthouse all set close together as in some old map—I recognize in the blue-coated man with the mass of white shirt the pilot I went fishing with, and I am full of disquiet and of excitement, and I am melancholy because I have not made more and better verses."

Out of these experiences, and this willingness to believe, came his 1893 collection of poems, *Crossways*. Most of the sixteen poems deal with the supernatural and mystical worlds. One of the most striking is his fairy tour of County Sligo in "The Stolen Child," which introduces a theme that Yeats returns to time and time again: the nearness of the mystical world to this one. As he writes in *The Celtic Twilight*, "Indeed, there are times when the worlds are so near together that it seems as if our earthly chattels were no more than the shadows of things beyond."

Yeats found a fellow believer in his Uncle George and his uncle's longtime servant Mary Battle, who was blessed with what Yeats called "second sight" (or, as others called it, intuition and common sense). For instance, Battle would set the table for an extra person well before Pollexfen would show up with an unexpected guest. One morning when she brought him a shirt to put on, she noticed a bloodstain on the front. After getting another shirt, she sent him off to work. Crossing a rock wall, Pollexfen slipped and cut himself in the exact spot where Battle had seen the blood. When he returned and told her, she realized that the first shirt was actually spotless. Yeats claimed that much of *The Celtic Twilight* "is but her daily speech."

To test their own extrasensory perception, Yeats and his Uncle George would walk along the shore experimenting:

> *There are some high sandhills and low cliffs, and I adopted the practice of walking by the seashore while he walked on cliff or sandhill; I, without speaking, would imagine the symbol, and he would notice what passed before his mind's eye, and in a short time he would practically never fail of the appropriate vision.*

Lissadell House

Yeats's mysticism was balanced by a love of the natural world and a growing interest in the culture of wealth and privilege. He found nature throughout Sligo; he found wealth and privilege at the home of the Gore-Booth sisters, ❸ Lissadell House. Situated on a bluff overlooking the placid waters of Drumcliff Bay, Lissadell House provided a glimpse into the life of the Anglo-

Lissadell House.

Irish Ascendancy (the rich Protestant landowners), a subject that would fascinate Yeats for years.

The Gore-Booth family lived in a gray limestone Greek Revival house twelve miles north of Sligo. Both Yeats and his brother Jack visited Lissadell as boys for cricket matches and horse racing. During 1894 and 1895, Yeats stayed there, describing it as "an exceedingly impressive house inside with a great sitting room as high as a church and all things in good taste; outside it is grey, square and bare yet set amid delightful grounds." While a guest there, Yeats led the life of the aristocracy: riding through the township of Lissadell and Drumcliff (although Yeats was a notably timid horseman), ice skating on Lough Gill with hot coffee on the shore afterward, and lounging around the estate.

Yeats developed close relationships with daughters Constance and Eva—particularly Eva, in whom he enjoyed the comfort of a confidante when he was mooning over Maud Gonne. Eva, a poet and artist in her own right, moved to Manchester in 1897 and crusaded tirelessly for the rights of the women who worked in the factories and mills there.

Her older sister, Constance, enrolled in the Slade Art School of London and then moved to Paris to continue her studies. There she met a Polish count, Casimir Markievicz, whom she married in 1901. After settling in Dublin in 1903, Constance Markievicz became close to the poet AE, even acting in his 1907 production of *Deirdre*. Little by little she became involved in politics, joining the Inghinidhe na hEireann, or Daughters of Erin (the Dublin women's version of Sinn Féin).

In April 1916, Constance was in Boland's Mill in Dublin with a gun in her hand and Ireland in her heart as part of the Easter Rebellion. Although

sentenced to die for her part in the uprising, she was released a year later and became the first woman elected to the British House of Commons. She later served her new government as the first minister of labour in the Irish Free State. A statue of her stands in a place of honor on St. Stephen's Green in Dublin.

Lough Gill

As the largest lake in that section of Sligo, ❹ Lough Gill was a favorite spot for adventures such as ice

The beautiful Gore-Booth sisters. Constance is on the left, Eva on the right.

skating with the Gore-Booths, but Yeats made solo expeditions there as well. Perhaps the most famous was his hike to camp out in ❺ **Slish Wood**, a wooded section on the southern shore of the lake:

> *I told [my uncle] I was going to walk round Lough Gill and sleep in a wood. I did not tell him all my object, for I was nursing a new ambition. My father had read to me some passage out of* Walden, *and I planned to live some day in a cottage on a little island called Innisfree, and Innisfree was opposite Slish Wood where I meant to sleep.*

The island of ❻ **Innisfree** is only one of the twenty-two islands that dot the shoreline of Lough Gill, but it is famous now because of the poem Yeats was inspired to write.

In *Reveries*, Yeats writes that he set out from Sligo in the evening and reached the woods a few hours later. He had trouble sleeping that night because he was afraid a ranger might discover him, and he'd have no good explanation for being there. Years later, he mused on the adventure:

> *I thought that having conquered bodily desire and the inclination of my mind towards women and*

Yeats hoped to live on this tiny island and make Lough Gill his Walden Pond. Instead, he celebrated the island in one of his most famous poems.

The Irish Transcendentalists

Yeats was not the only Irish writer with an artistic or philosophic connection to the American Transcendentalists. AE and J. M. Synge were also influenced by the work of Ralph Waldo Emerson and Henry David Thoreau. American Transcendentalism was centered on the idea that spirituality can be located within an individual and in the natural world as opposed to strictly within organized religion. Although it was a much more spiritual and philosophical movement than the Irish Literary Revival, it provided the Revival with artistic formulas and political strategies. As with the Revival, many of Transcendentalism's ideas and theories were developed and tested in the more intimate setting of clubs and society gatherings before being published. The two movements had similar success with poetry inspired by a love for the natural world. Above all, the two shared a common precursor: both were influenced by the nature-inspired poetry of William Wordsworth, the visionary writings of William Blake, and the radical philosophy of Samuel Taylor Coleridge.

On the political front, scholar Declan Kiberd describes a major difference between the two movements:

> *What makes the Irish Renaissance such a fascinating case is the knowledge that the cultural revival preceded and in many ways enabled the political revolution that followed. This is quite the opposite of the American experience, in which the attainment of cultural autonomy by Whitman and Emerson followed the political Declaration of Independence by fully seventy-five years.*

Henry David Thoreau.

Slish and Cullentra Woods: The Millennium Forests Project

Ireland remains one of the most deforested countries in Europe, but as a lover of the woods, Yeats would be pleased with a recent government project. To celebrate the millennium, Ireland took up a suggestion offered by Lady Gregory some hundred years before. In 1899, she began advocating the planting of trees and planted many trees on the property at Coole. In 2000, the government designated more than fifteen hundred acres of native woods as People's Millennium Forests. In sixteen different sites, the government planted a native tree for each area household. Every household was then sent a certificate listing the type of tree and location, so it could track down its specific tree.

In addition to reforesting these areas with native seeds, the project included educational programs, a traveling exhibition, a video and accompanying book, training programs, and a website featuring information about Ireland's ancient connections with trees and the recent history of its forests.

The Millennium Forest for the county of Sligo lies on the southern shore of Lough Gill, very near Innisfree, and is called Cullentra Woods. It consists of three separate sites along the lakeshore. The trees planted include birch, symbol of a new start; oak, one of the "nobles of the wood"; and ash, one of ancient Ireland's magical trees. (It is said that Saint Patrick drove the snakes out of Ireland with an ash stick.)

83

love, I should live, as Thoreau lived, seeking wisdom. There was a story in the county history of a tree that had once grown upon that island guarded by some terrible monster and borne the food of the gods. A young girl pined for the fruit and told her lover to kill the monster and carry the fruit away. He did as he had been told, but tasted the fruit; and when he reached the mainland where she waited for him, he was dying of its powerful virtue. And from sorrow and from remorse she too ate of it and died. I do not remember whether I chose the island because of its beauty or for the story's sake, but I was twenty-two or three before I gave up the dream.

However, before he "gave up the dream," he was reminded of the island while walking through London:

I still had the ambition, formed in Sligo in my teens, of living in imitation of Thoreau on Innisfree, a little island in Lough Gill, and when walking through Fleet Street very homesick I heard a little tinkle of water and saw a fountain in a shop-window which balanced a little ball upon its

From Dooney Rock, the view extends across Lough Gill to Ben Bulben in the distance.

jet, and began to remember lake water. From the sudden remembrance came my poem "Innisfree," my first lyric with anything in its rhythm of my own music. I had begun to loosen rhythm as an escape from rhetoric and from that emotion of the crowd that rhetoric brings.

Yeats's poem "Innisfree," with its sense of the poet's music in the rhythm, has become perhaps his most recognized. Its long vowel sounds and repetitions, along with the visual imagery, have helped countless students to commit its three rhyming stanzas to memory.

Lough Gill has a number of other Yeats associations as well. Just west of Slish Wood and Innisfree stands an enormous formation called ❼ **Dooney Rock.** At its base are a car park and a set of trails that lead around the rock and up to its summit, which offers unparalleled views of Lough Gill across to Ben Bulben mountain. The site is the setting for Yeats's poem "The Fiddler of Dooney" (1899). When Yeats's fiddler plays his songs from a book he bought at a Sligo fair, "people dance like a wave upon a sea."

Perhaps no place along the shores of Lough Gill was as magical to Yeats (and to the modern-day traveler) as ❽ **Hazelwood.** This section of woods along Half Moon Bay glimmers in the morning light but darkens with the afternoon shade, when it becomes an enchanting place where one might just come across a fairy. In "The Song of Wandering Aengus" (1899), Yeats describes a man who is put under a spell by the sight of a fairy along the Hazelwood shore. The man, grown old searching for the fairy, imagines finally finding her and "walk[ing] among the long dappled grass," plucking "the silver apples of the moon" and "the golden apples of the sun." Just what those silver and golden apples symbolize has led to much

contemplation, but to many Irish minds, Yeats's vision of a land of "long dappled grass" stands for the Ireland of the past—the Ireland of Celtic mythology, the subject of so much of Yeats's early work.

Hazelwood is also now a particularly interesting stop for its sculpture park at Half Moon Bay. Built as the nation's

One of the peculiar doorways that make Hazelwood so distinctive.

Measuring almost forty-five feet tall, this waterfall tucked into the side of the mountain is compared to a marvelous white stag by Yeats in "Towards Break of Day."

first sculpture trail, this footpath beside the lake brings the walker into sudden encounters with giant wooden men and strange arched doorways. The effect can be surreal, but it makes for a pleasant amble along the water.

Another nearby magical place for Yeats was the ❾ Glencar Waterfall in County Leitrim. This nearly forty-five-foot waterfall makes its first appearance in one of Yeats's earliest poems, "The Stolen Child" (1889) and becomes a central image in his later poem "Towards Break of Day" (1921). In the latter, the poet dreams of the waterfall and can feel the cold spray, while his lover dreams of "the marvellous stag of Arthur, / That lofty white stag, leap / From mountain steep to steep." The poem considers whether the cascading water of the falls of the one dream is the "double" of the white stag leaping from rock to rock of his lover's dream. Yeats's process of creating public symbol from intimate landscape is made manifest: each stream, mountaintop, lakeshore, or wood is filled with private meaning or personal truth.

Ben Bulben

As the most prominent landmark in the area, with its steep limestone cliffs and jutting nose, ⑩ **Ben Bulben** has attracted the attention of poets and storytellers throughout the ages. In *The Celtic Twilight*, Yeats describes the mountain as the accepted home of the fairies:

A little north of the town of Sligo, on the southern side of Ben Bulben, some hundreds of feet above the plain, is a small white square in the limestone. No mortal has ever touched it with his hand; no sheep or goat has ever browsed grass beside it. There is no more inaccessible place upon the earth, and few more encircled by awe to the deep considering. It is the door of faery-land. In the middle of

According to legend, somewhere in the side of Ben Bulben is the secret door to fairyland.

night it swings open, and the unearthly troop rushes out. All night the gay rabble sweep to and fro across the land, invisible to all, unless perhaps where, in some more than commonly "gentle" place—Drumcliff or Drum-a-hair—the nightcapped heads of faery-doctors may be thrust from their doors to see what mischief the "gentry" are doing.

This mountain was a favorite place for Yeats to hike, and it has become a literary pilgrimage site. Its summit, 1,730 feet above Drumcliff, offers views across Sligo Bay to Knocknarea in the south and around to Bundoran in the north.

Toward the end of his life, Yeats envisioned a return to Ben Bulben, if only poetically. In "Under Ben Bulben" (1939), one of his last poems, he brings the reader back to the fairies of Sligo who had appeared in much earlier poems such as "The Hosting of the Sidhe" (1889).

After making the case for the power of public art generally and Irish art specifically, Yeats ends this opening poem of the collection *Last Poems* with a description of his own funeral:

Under bare Ben Bulben's head
In Drumcliff churchyard Yeats is laid,
An ancestor was rector there
Long years ago, a church stands near,
By the road an ancient cross.
No marble, no conventional phrase;
On limestone quarried near the spot
By his command these words are cut:

> *Cast a cold eye*
> *On life, on death.*
> *Horseman, pass by!*

These very words are engraved on the limestone tablet that lies to the left of the paved parking lot in front of ❶ **Drumcliff Church.** The church sits on the site of a monastery founded in 574 A.D. by Saint Columba. In 1809, stones from the ruined monastery were used to build the church. Yeats's great-grandfather served as the rector in the early nineteenth century.

With its sweeping view of the surrounding countryside, the top of Ben Bulben is a prime picnic spot.

The churchyard is a quiet, peaceful place with views of Ben Bulben through the trees, a fitting resting place for this poet of the woods and the hills. While the tour buses in the parking lot and the Yeats gift shop and café may detract from the churchyard's serenity, there are still private places here where one can contemplate Yeats's remarkable contribution to Irish literature.

Sligo: Preserving Heritage

For the young Yeats, Sligo Town meant a big house just outside the town center called the **⑫ Merville House.** This was the residence of his maternal grandparents, William and Elizabeth Pollexfen. The house was huge and filled with fascinating artifacts from William's maritime career. Yeats said that his second-oldest memory was of this house: "The house was so big that there was always a room to hide in, and I had a red pony and a garden where I could wander, and there were two dogs to follow at my heels, one white with some black spots on his head and the other with long black hair all over him."

Although his memories of his grandparents' house remained vivid for much of his life, Yeats seems to have been more influenced by the surrounding countryside and makes no real mention of the town, other than

Drumcliff Church, built on the site of an ancient monastery.

After Yeats's death in France, his body was buried in this grave next to Drumcliff Church.

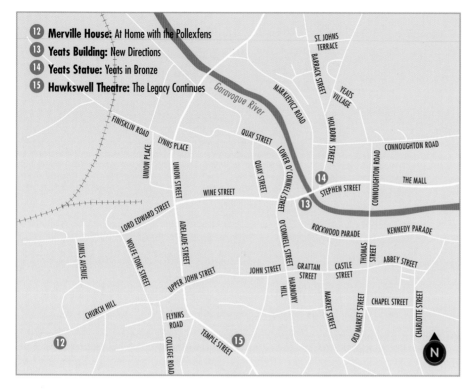

12 **Merville House:** At Home with the Pollexfens
13 **Yeats Building:** New Directions
14 **Yeats Statue:** Yeats in Bronze
15 **Hawkswell Theatre:** The Legacy Continues

Phase II of the multiphase-plan includes a renovation and extension of the building to become the Yeats Resource and Cultural Center, with exhibition spaces, a video room, a bookshop, and a café.

The center gives the Yeats Society of Sligo comfortable facilities for its annual Yeats summer school, its winter session, and the Yeats festival in August. The society and the summer school were founded by a group of Sligo citizens who wanted to do something in honor of Yeats. They decided on a summer school dedicated to the rigorous and in-depth study of Yeats among the surroundings

describing visiting friends of his grandparents'. His imagination was much more gripped by places such as the tiny fishing village of Rosses Point.

Sligo seems intent on preserving the memory of not just William Butler Yeats but also his brother Jack, who put "a little thought of Sligo" in each of his paintings, and the fiery patriot and stateswoman Constance Markievicz.

The center of activity is the **13** **Yeats Building**, in the middle of town. Just over Hyde Bridge and alongside the River Garavogue, the building houses the Yeats Society Library, the Sligo Art Gallery, and a photographic exhibit detailing much of Yeats's private and public life.

that contributed so much to his development as a poet.

The school offers two full weeks of morning lectures, evening seminars, tours, special nighttime presentations, and lots of time to discuss almost all aspects of Yeats. The list of past and present faculty associated with the summer school is impressive, including Edward Said, Seamus Heaney, Thomas Kinsella, Richard Ellmann, Helen Vendler, and many others.

Just across the river on Stephen Street, in front of the Ulster Bank building in Sligo, is a **14** **statue of Yeats.** When visiting Sweden to receive the Nobel Prize for Literature, Yeats commented that the Stockholm Royal Palace reminded him of the Ulster Bank of Sligo. In

This interpretation of Yeats and his work stands in front of the Ulster Bank of Sligo.

Yeats may be the only writer in the world with a soccer club named after him. The Yeats United Football Club was formed in 1989 out of two separate clubs and plays in the town of Carney between Lissadell and Drumcliff.

members of the Irish Literary Revival. The tourist office is well stocked with maps and books, and the staff can help travelers find a room for the night or the route to the top of Ben Bulben. It is a good place to get oriented before heading out on the Yeats Trail, a self-guided, signposted tour of Sligo leading to many of the sites covered in this chapter.

For Yeats, though, Sligo was not about visiting public sites. Sligo was a place where he could get away from the busy metropolises of London and Dublin. It provided an opportunity to explore the secret places in nature, where the mystical realm was not so far from the physical one. The natural beauty of Sligo influenced Yeats much in the same way that County Wicklow instilled a sense of solitude and loneliness in its native son J. M. Synge.

1989, to honor the fiftieth anniversary of his death, the townspeople erected this statue by Rowan Gillespie in front of the bank.

Back on the other side of the river, up on Temple Street, is the ⓯ Hawkswell Theatre, right next to the tourist office. The theater, named for Yeats's play *The Hawk's Well*, offers a rich season, including plays by

Chapter 6

County Wicklow
South and West and South Again

Mere minutes from the center of Dublin, the hills near Sugarloaf Mountain have changed little since Synge roamed through them as a young man.

Prelude

Still south I went and west and south again,
Through Wicklow from the morning till the night,
And far from cities, and the sights of men,
Lived with the sunshine and the moon's delight.

I knew the stars, the flowers, and the birds
The grey and wintry sides of many glens,
And did but half remember human words,
In converse with the mountains, moors, and fens.

—**J. M. Synge**

As far back as the sixteenth century, the British government referred to the area immediately surrounding Dublin, in which English authority ruled absolutely, as "the Pale." Originally referring to a fortified area surrounding the center of British power, Dublin Castle, the Pale implied a relatively stable and cultured existence a comfortable remove from the uncivilized Irish countryside.

The area just south of Dublin, now known as County Wicklow, was definitely outside the Pale. Running from the palatial estate of Powerscourt in the north to the coastal town of Arklow in the south, Wicklow encompasses granite mountains, long narrow valleys, and secret glens. Although it is only a dozen miles from downtown Dublin, it seems a world away. County Wicklow's population of about 120,000 is spread over nearly eight hundred square miles. The major cities of Bray, Wicklow, and Arklow are along the coast, while the interior is dotted with small towns and villages such as Roundwood and Glendalough.

Running north to south through the county are the Wicklow Mountains, a range of smooth-topped granite

Glanmore Castle was built by Synge's great-grandfather, but Synge was never in line to inherit it; he could visit only as a guest.

peaks with deep valleys cut by erosion. Much of the wilderness is heath and peat, with occasional groves of oaks or, in places where the government has reforested, conifers. The county boasts high barren mountains, plateaus covered with grass and rocks, and wooded glens hidden in back valleys. With twenty-eight miles of coastline on the eastern perimeter, County Wicklow calls itself the garden of Ireland.

Synge's Wicklow

County Wicklow, "far from cities, and the sights of men," often tempted J. M. Synge away from Dublin. The Synges had ties to the area, and in many ways he felt at home here. Although the material for his best-known book came from the Aran Islands and his most famous play was set in County Mayo, much of his work is infused with Wicklow's rugged landscape and the grittiness of daily life there.

One of the county's biggest influences on Synge, both as a place to visit and as a symbol of his heritage as a Protestant landowner, was ❶ Glanmore Castle, near the town of Ashford. This large Gothic castle at the center of more than one thousand acres of prime Wicklow property was built by Synge's great-grandfather, Francis, in the early nineteenth century. Unfortunately for Synge, this inherited wealth was burdened by debt and spread thinly among Francis's many descendants. When Synge came of age, he received no huge estate or castle but merely an income of forty pounds a year: just enough, he told Yeats one time, to buy a new suit of clothes when he became too shabby.

In Synge's lifetime Glanmore Castle was owned by his uncle, who had saved the property from debt. The uncle rented a smaller house on the property, ❷ **Castle Kevin,** to Synge's mother. This cottage provided the Synge family with a summer home that was out of the city, close to friends and relatives, and in their beloved County Wicklow. Synge lived with his mother off and on, mostly during the summers, from 1892 to 1907. The house was eventually bought by Ann Saddlemeyer, a renowned Synge scholar, who sold it to the Irish poet Seamus Heaney, who used it as a writing retreat.

From Castle Kevin's central location near the town of Ashford, Synge could explore much of County Wicklow on foot. He came to know the people and the natural world of the remote and desolate glens, and these experiences colored all that he wrote.

Near Glanmore and Castle Kevin is the curiously named Devil's Glen, where Synge often rambled as a child. The glen was carved out by the Vartry River, which continues to flow through the bottom of the gorge. The area is now owned by a lumber company that manages the area as a recreational park and offers walking trails, picnic sites, and a woodland sculpture park.

The Wicklow influence is particularly noticeable in Synge's play *In the*

Shadow of the Glen. The plot, based on a story Synge heard on the Aran Islands, is set in the remote region of ❸ **Glenmalure,** up the valley of the Avonbeg River. The plot may be Aran, but the dialogue is pure Wicklow. As he writes in his program note to *The Playboy of the Western World,*

> *When I was writing "The Shadow of the Glen," some years ago, I got more aid than any learning could have given me from a chink in the floor of the old Wicklow house where I was staying, that let me hear what was being said by the servant girls in the kitchen. This matter, I think, is of importance, for in countries where the imagination of the people, and the language they use, is rich and living, it is possible for a writer to be rich and copious in his words, and at the same time to give the reality, which is the root of all poetry, in a comprehensive and natural form.*

Synge often walked in Devil's Glen as a child.

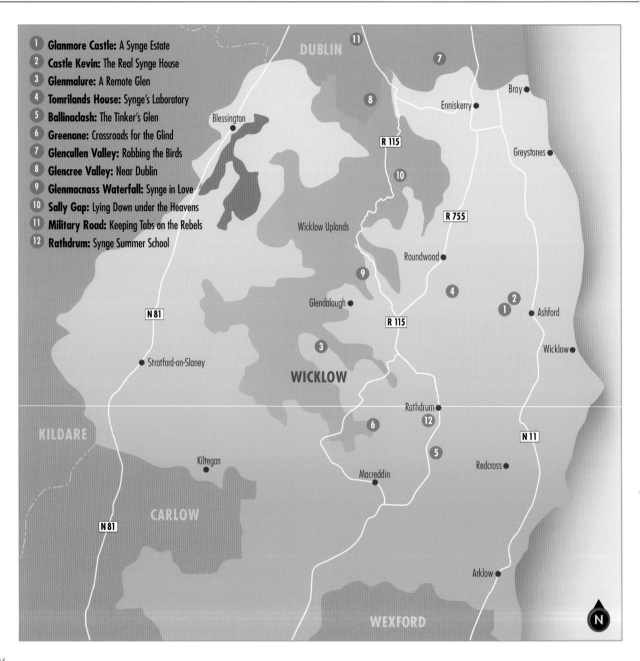

1. **Glanmore Castle:** A Synge Estate
2. **Castle Kevin:** The Real Synge House
3. **Glenmalure:** A Remote Glen
4. **Tomrilands House:** Synge's Laboratory
5. **Ballinaclash:** The Tinker's Glen
6. **Greenane:** Crossroads for the Glind
7. **Glencullen Valley:** Robbing the Birds
8. **Glencree Valley:** Near Dublin
9. **Glenmacnass Waterfall:** Synge in Love
10. **Sally Gap:** Lying Down under the Heavens
11. **Military Road:** Keeping Tabs on the Rebels
12. **Rathdrum:** Synge Summer School

DUBLIN

Blessington

R 115

Wicklow Uplands

R 755

Roundwood

Enniskerry

Bray

Greystones

Ashford

Wicklow

Glendalough

R 115

N 81

Stratford-on-Slaney

WICKLOW

Rathdrum

KILDARE

Kiltegan

Macreddin

Redcross

N 11

CARLOW

N 81

Arklow

WEXFORD

N

Eavesdropping on servant girls was typical of Synge's method. As he once told Yeats, he liked to make himself as inconspicuous as possible when gathering material for his work. Whether this meant listening through a chink in the floor or fading into a corner, Synge's strategy was to observe people unobtrusively in their daily interactions.

In this case, it was the Catholic servant girls at ❹ Tomrilands House, near Tomrilands Crossing, that provided the syntax and imagery of his Wicklow characters. Synge's mother rented the farm during the summer of 1902. Its location, between the village of Annamoe and familiar Synge haunts such as Castle Kevin and Glanmore Castle, provided an excellent base of operations: Synge could listen carefully to the servants in the kitchen and then roam up past Glendalough to the Wicklow Gap or north through Roundwood toward Sally Gap.

In addition to providing the lyrical Anglo-Irish language, Wicklow offered a unique geography and historical context that made it the perfect setting for many of Synge's plays. *In the Shadow of the Glen* is the story of a man who fakes being dead in order to catch his wife with her young lover. In the end, the wife leaves with a passing tinker, who offers her little more than poetry (but it's grand poetry):

> *Come along with me now, lady of the house, and it's not my blather you'll be hearing only, but you'll be hearing the herons crying out over the black lakes, and you'll be hearing the grouse and the owls with them, and the larks and the big thrushes when the days are warm.*

The story evokes a place so isolated and remote that a woman would conceivably spend a night alone with her dead husband in a tiny cottage. This is a far different

scenario from the funeral Synge portrays on Inis Meáin in *The Aran Islands*, where the whole community is not only rocked by deaths but wholly present and involved with funerals: "The coffin was still lying in front of the door, with the men and women of the family standing round beating it, and keening over it, in a great crowd of people."

Farther along the Avonbeg River, the town of ❺ Ballinaclash provides the setting for another of Synge's finest plays, *The Tinker's Wedding*. This play, which is reminiscent of George Moore's short story "Patchwork" from *The Untilled Field*, addresses the greed of the local clergy. As in "Patchwork," the local priest refuses to marry a couple unless they can pay his full fee for the ceremony. In this case the couple, a tinker and his young but ambitious betrothed, negotiate a deal involving tin cans. When the groom's drunken mother steals the little money they had and ruins their plans, the deal falls apart; the play ends with the priest tied up and stuffed in a sack. To add further controversy, the couple questions the priest's importance in their lives. The mother, Mary Byrne, sums things up this way: "It's little need we ever had of the like of you to get us our bit to eat, and our bit to drink, and our time of love when we were young men and women, and were fine to look at."

The Tinker's Wedding was so controversial that it was never produced in Synge's lifetime; it was first staged in London in 1909. Yeats felt, and Synge agreed, that stirring up the pot after *Playboy* would not be prudent. *The Tinker's Wedding* was not produced in Ireland until the centennial of Synge's birth, in 1971.

For *The Well of the Saints*, Synge took another story from the Aran Islands and set it in Wicklow. In 1905 the Abbey Theatre produced the play, set at the

An isolated house like this one provides the setting for Synge's play about a man faking his own death in order to catch his wife cheating.

crossroads of ❻ **Greenane,** just downstream from Glenmalure on the Avonbeg River. A visiting priest offers to restore sight to a pair of old Wicklow vagrants with water carried from the holy well at the Church of the Four Beautiful Saints on Inis Mór (see chapter 3). Although they continually bicker and fight, the couple have a lasting marriage, based perhaps on mutual need and the sense that they are different from others.

Of course, sight changes their perceptions and expectations, and they are soon estranged. Only when they have lost their sight again do they reunite. In addition, the town's opinion of the two changes as their fortunes change: two curmudgeonly old people who see and criticize everything that passes in front of their eyes are not as acceptable as the blind, oblivious fools they had been.

The importance of sight is a theme that runs through much of Synge's work. In *Playboy*, the villagers react very differently to the sin recounted in poetic detail than to the sin they witness. *The Aran Islands* is filled with visual imagery that reflects mood and tone, and County Wicklow inspired some of Synge's best poetry. Whereas Yeats inscribed the landscape with his own private symbolism, Synge quietly observed and strove to interpret what he saw.

Synge's Poetry of Wicklow: Intimate and Interactive

Although Synge's reputation rightfully rests with his plays and *The Aran Islands*, he did write poetry from time to time. While often lacking the vitality of the Anglo-Irish speech that infuses much of his work, his poetry occasionally offers a surprisingly intimate portrait of the writer's connection to this place.

For example, in "To the Oaks of Glencree" (1909), Synge envisions the tree as his lover, only to ultimately turn on the idea of an "eternal love":

> *My arms are around you, and I lean*
> *Against you, while the lark*
> *Sings over us, and golden lights, and green*
> *Shadows are on your bark.*
> *There'll come a season when you'll stretch*
> *Black boards to cover me;*
> *Then in Mount Jerome I will lie, poor wretch,*
> *With worms eternally.*

The Mount Jerome of the poem is Dublin's forty-seven-acre Protestant cemetery, where many of the town's most prominent citizens were buried. Synge ended up there, just as he had forecast.

Only ten or so miles from the center of Dublin, the ❼ **Glencullen valley** is a gateway to the more remote and isolated regions of Wicklow. Synge reiterates the idea of cycles and lives in "In Glencullen" (1909), in which he contrasts his lifespan with the shorter one of birds in a meditation on his relationship to nature:

> *Thrush, linnet, stare and wren,*
> *Brown lark beside the sun,*
> *Take thought of kestrel, sparrow-hawk,*
> *Birdlime and roving gun.*
>
> *You great-great-grandchildren*
> *Of birds I've listened to,*
> *I think I robbed your ancestors*
> *When I was young as you.*

This portrait of Synge was painted around 1916 by Benjamin T. Bailey.

The Irish Tinkers, or Travelers

Integral to Synge's childhood landscape were the "tinkers," or travelers: groups of families and workers who traveled from town fair to town fair, hawking their wares and services. Their nickname, "tinker," comes from the Irish word for tinsmith, *tinceard*. The tinkers in *The Tinker's Wedding* make their living by crafting tin cans and doing light metalwork.

The Irish travelers were also talented musicians and poets. Studies of a secret language they used, called Shelta, show some connections to a separate class of poets and storytellers that wandered the Irish countryside.

Irish travelers often live in these distinctive caravans.

Although occasionally confused with the European or English gypsies, these peripatetic bands form a distinct ethnic group today of more than twenty thousand in the Irish Republic (less than 1 percent of the population). With modernization and industrialization, the need for tinsmithing and traveling musicians has greatly diminished, so many have given up their nomadic existence and settled down.

In these poems, Synge is not only in nature but of nature. He is part of nature, and his life is intertwined with the trees and birds he sees. Because the tree will provide the boards for his coffin, its fate is inextricably linked to his. Similarly, the birds were forced to give their young to sustain Synge's younger self. However, the tree continues to grow and is immortalized, and the birds have survived to come into contact with Synge again. Although nature is eternal for Synge, it is not unchanging.

The Wicklow glens were also a place to share with special people. After Synge joined the management team of the Abbey Theatre, he fell in love with one of the actresses, Molly Allgood, and they were soon engaged. However, to avoid censure by Synge's mother (Molly was of a different class) and the Abbey Theatre members, they kept their trysts private.

After *Playboy* enjoyed a wildly successful opening in London in 1907, Synge spent a blissful two weeks with

Molly and her sister in a cottage in the ❽ **Glencree valley,** which lies at the north end of Wicklow and was one of the two valleys Synge could easily explore from his homes in Rathgar, Rathfarnham, and Dun Laoghaire.

His poetry from this time, still rooted in the local landscape, is infused with a simple joy, as evidenced by "Queens" (1909), in which Synge describes sitting with Molly and enjoying the "seven dog-days we let pass / Naming Queens in Glenmacnass." The

❾ **Glenmacnass waterfall,** which inspired Synge, is one of the more impressive water features in Wicklow. In "Queens," Synge turns from Irish legends (he was working on a new play, *Deirdre*, based on an ancient Celtic myth) to proclaim Molly the new Irish queen:

> *Yet these are rotten—I ask their pardon—*
> *And we've the sun on rock and garden,*
> *These are rotten, so you're the Queen*
> *Of all the living, or have been.*

Glenmacnass waterfall.

After the Glenmacnass waterfall, the valley broadens and the river meanders down to the town of Laragh.

Wicklow Today: Still Remote, Still Spectacular

Even with the economy roaring and new construction proceeding at a frenzied pace, the wide-open spaces of Wicklow still feel removed from the center of Dublin. A visitor can drive Route R 115 to ⑩ Sally Gap, where Synge often hiked and enjoyed "lying down under the heavens," and stand at the top of Sally Gap and look for miles in every direction without seeing a soul.

The villages of Annamoe, Roundwood, and Glendalough are not much different today than when Synge wandered through them on his walks. He often came to town on market day to photograph both the locals and the tinkers. He made a point of talking to people and often heard stories, both bad and good, about his ancestors.

But for the modern-day literature lover, the key destination is the town of ⑫ Rathdrum, where the annual Synge summer school is in session every August. The school, like the Yeats summer school in Sligo, offers two weeks of lectures, small-group discussions, and opportunities to explore the writer's world. Highlights of recent programs include lectures by Irish scholars such as Declan Kiberd and Nobel laureate Seamus Heaney, as well as tours to Devil's Glen, Glenmalure, and Tomrilands House. For two weeks, the quiet, hidden places of the county are visited by fans of the playwright from Wicklow who made his mark on the public stage of Dublin.

The Military Road

Wicklow's terrain is perfect for getting lost in, or for not being found in the first place—a fact well known by both rebels and authorities. In 1798, during the attempted uprising against the British government in Ireland, Fenians (Irish rebels fighting to oust the British from Ireland) used the hills as hideouts and secret bases. The British decided to build a forty-five-mile road into the area to help them find the insurgents. This became known as the ⑪ Military Road. Few local civilians would work on the road, so English soldiers were employed for a shilling a day; overseers were paid five shillings. By 1809, more than fourteen thousand pounds had been spent and five barracks had been built to house soldiers protecting the road. By 1815, however, the road had already lost some of its strategic importance because the Napoleonic Wars had ended and the chances of the French supporting an Irish insurrection had faded.

The road begins in the Dublin suburb of Rathfarnham, the birthplace of Synge, and winds up through Killakee and over the Featherbed Mountain to Glencree, ending at Aughavannagh. It is a stunning scenic route, now favored by bikers and hikers.

Chapter 7

Dublin
The Public Stage

Once a dirty and poverty-stricken city, Dublin is now one of the most vibrant cultural capitals in Europe.

The town is as full as ever of "characters," all created by each other.

—Wilfred Sheen

Two historic Dublin events unfolded on very public stages not far from each other. One was a purely literary event influenced by politics; the other was a political event shaped in part by literature: the 1907 riots at the Abbey Theatre over J. M. Synge's *The Playboy of the Western World*, and, just a few streets away, the 1916 Easter Rising, headquartered in Dublin's General Post Office. Both were so symbolic of the Irish Literary Revival, and so drastically affected the movement, that much of the Revival can be described in terms of its relationship to one or both of these events.

Dublin was by no means merely a blank stage upon which these two great dramas were played out. Especially in the case of the Revival, the city played a very prominent role. As the birthplace of Yeats, Synge, and Shaw; the home to many Revival writers; the center for numerous clubs and societies; and the political and social capital of Ireland, Dublin had a tremendous influence over what was read, watched, and discussed. In many ways, what was conceived in the intimacy of private homes and secret places in the west of Ireland had its public birth in Dublin.

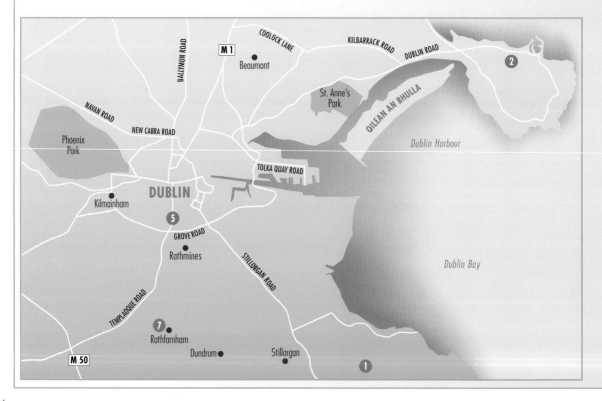

1. **5 Sandymount Avenue, Sandycove:** Yeats's Birthplace
2. **Howth:** Yeats by the Sea
3. **44 York Street:** John Yeats's Studio
4. **40 Harcourt Street:** Erasmus High School
5. **418 Harold's Cross Road:** Yeats's Suburban Home
6. **Kildare Street:** The Dublin Metropolitan School of Art
7. **2 Newtown Villas, Rathfarnham:** Synge's Birthplace
8. **85 Upper Dorset Street:** O'Casey's Birthplace
9. **35 Mountjoy Square:** O'Casey's Apartment
10. **42 Pearse Street:** Antient Concert Rooms
11. **South King Street:** The Gaiety Theatre
12. **Clarendon Street:** St. Teresa's Total Abstinence Hall
13. **Molesworth Street:** Molesworth Hall
14. **26 Lower Abbey Street:** Abbey Theatre
15. **Pearse Street:** The Queen's Theatre
16. **O'Connell Street:** General Post Office
17. **Dublin Castle:** Symbol of Britain's Power
18. **8 Ely Place:** Dublin Theosophical Society
19. **4 Ely Place:** George Moore's Home
20. **15 Ely Place:** Oliver St. John Gogarty's Home
21. **82 and 84 Merrion Square:** Home to Yeats and AE
22. **19–20 Lower Mount Street:** Elpis Private Hospital
23. **Parnell Square North, Charlemont House:** Hugh Lane Gallery
24. **18 Parnell Square:** Dublin Writers Museum
25. **Duke Street:** Duke Pub
26. **Merrion Square West:** National Gallery
27. **Kildare Street:** National Library
28. **Grand Canal Docks:** Sean O'Casey Bridge

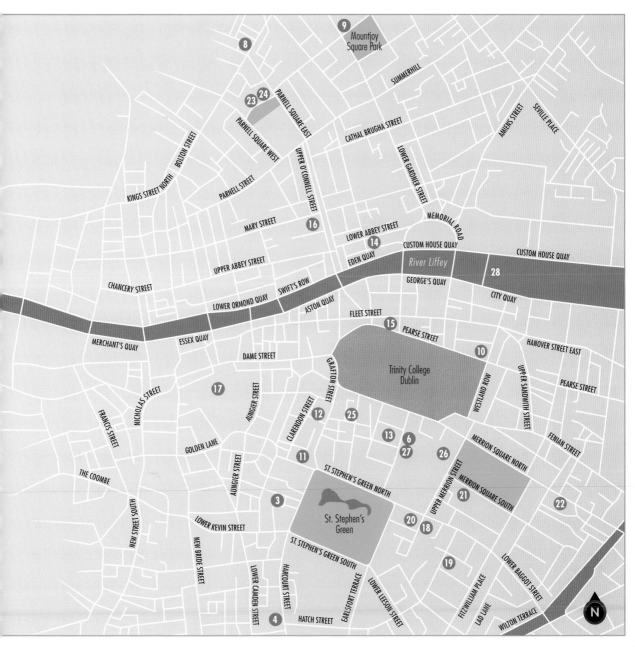

A City Steeped in Beauty and Tragedy

Dublin, overlooked on the south by the Wicklow Mountains, bisected by the River Liffey, and ringed by forty miles of beaches, was built according to the rules of eighteenth-century design. The city's Gaelic name is Dubh linn, or "dark pool," likely for the River Liffey, which flows through the center of the town. On both sides of the river, wide streets run north to south, with major parks laid out in neat rectangles. Some of the most dramatic moments of the Revival, particularly the *Playboy* riots and the Easter Rising, occurred north of the river; the southern side contains many homes, schools, and workplaces of those involved in the Revival.

Predominantly Catholic, Dublin was ruled by Protestant bank owners, industry tycoons, and Unionist politicians for much its pre–Irish Free State history. In 1902 it had a population of nearly three hundred thousand and was both England's bastion of power in Ireland and Ireland's cultural center.

Dublin is very much a city of contrasts: although architecturally beautiful, it was home to some of the worst poverty in the world at the end of the nineteenth century, arguably as bad as that of Calcutta. It has nurtured three winners of the Nobel Prize for Literature, yet it is just as well known for literary censorship that has sent many of its best writers into exile and banned the very books that bring so many literary fans and historians to the city.

Childhood by the Sea

South of the Liffey is the quiet seaside village of Sandycove. In a nondescript house at what is now ❶ **5 Sandymount Avenue,** William Butler Yeats was born on June 13, 1865, to a law student (who was a painter at heart) and the daughter of a wealthy Sligo merchant. The Yeats family lived in this house for just two years before moving to London. The town has memorialized Yeats with a plaque on the house and a statue of the poet on the town green. Sandycove may be best known, however, for the round tower where novelist James Joyce lived. He describes it in the first chapter of his stream-of-consciousness novel *Ulysses.*

After a London sojourn of fourteen years, the Yeats family returned to Dublin because Yeats's father felt he could get more business as a painter there. They settled in ❷ **Howth,** situated on a peninsula nine miles north of the city. They first lived in

Solidly suburban, 5 Sandymount Avenue (the door on the right) was the birthplace of Yeats.

Balscadden Cottage and later in a house on Kilrock Road called Island View. Although they lived in Howth for only two years, this was Yeats's formative period, and his description of his experiences there speaks to the town's lasting impact on his imagination:

> Our house for the first year or so was on the top of a cliff so that in stormy weather the spray would soak my bed at night, for I had taken the glass out of the window, sash and all. A literary passion for the open air was to last me a few years. Then for another year we had a house overlooking the harbour where the one great sight was the going and coming of the fishing fleet. We had one regular servant, a fisherman's wife, and the occasional help of a big, red-faced girl who ate a whole pot of jam while my mother was at church and accused me of it. . . .
>
> At other times, I would sleep among the rhododendrons and rocks in the wilder part of the grounds of Howth Castle. After a while my father said I must stay indoors half the night, meaning I should get some sleep in my bed; but I, knowing that I would be too sleepy and comfortable to get up again, used to sit over the kitchen fire till half the night was gone.

It was also during these years that Yeats began collecting some of the stories he would include in his first volume of prose, *The Celtic Twilight*. The stories told to his mother by their maid make up much of "Village Ghosts." Howth certainly was an interesting place to live, with ghosts and demons on nearly every street into town:

> To approach the village at night a timid man requires great strategy. A man was once heard complaining, "By the cross of Jesus! how shall I

The local bird population in Sandycove has less respect for Yeats than he is due.

WILLIAM BUTLER YEATS
BORN IN SANDYMOUNT
13TH JUNE 1865

go? If I pass the hill of Dunboy, old captain Burney may look out on me. If I go round by the water, and up by the steps, there is the headless one and another on the quays, and a new one under the old churchyard wall. If I go right round the other way, Mrs. Steward is appearing at the Hillside Gate, and the devil himself is in the Hospital Lane."

Yeats strikes an almost disappointed note when he compares these ghosts with the ones he hears of in the west, however. Instead of haunting and wreaking havoc, these ghosts do errands: "These H—— spirits have a gloomy, matter-of-fact way with them. They come to

As a child, Yeats spent nights prowling around Howth Castle or sleeping among the rhododendrons.

announce a death, to fulfil some obligation, to revenge a wrong, to pay their bills even—as did a fisherman's daughter the other day—and then hasten to their rest. All things they do decently and in order."

A Portrait of the Poet as a Young Man

When not haunting old castles or being disappointed by ghosts, Yeats went to high school in Dublin. Although the family lived in Howth, young Willie traveled into the city each morning with his father to his studio at ❸ 44 York Street, breakfasted there, and then walked around the corner to ❹ Erasmus High School, 40 Harcourt Street. Yeats describes the school:

I found a bleak eighteenth-century house, a small playing-field full of mud and pebbles, fenced by an iron railing, and opposite a long hoarding [billboard] and a squalid, ornamental railway station. Here, as I soon found, nobody gave a thought to decorum. We worked in a din of voices. . . . On the other hand there was no bullying and I had not thought it possible that boys could work so hard.

The school was geared toward preparing students for careers in the clergy or in offices, and thus was not necessarily suited to a budding poet. Yeats took courses in mathematics, the classics, natural history (he brought in live specimens in matchboxes), and, of course, English literature. He was merely an adequate student: "What could I, who never worked when I was not interested, do with a history lesson that was but a column of seventy dates? I was worst of all at literature, for we read Shakespeare for his grammar exclusively." He did well in math but had trouble memorizing the 150 lines of Virgil required each night. While he was not drawn to any sport (one colleague remarked that he couldn't remember Yeats ever running or picking up a ball), he did play a lot of chess. He even put a chessboard on his knees and secretly played with another student during math class.

Despite earning a prize in English and a certificate of exemplary conduct, Yeats was unable to win admission to Trinity College. For fear of upsetting his father, Yeats did not tell him that his test scores, particularly in math and the classics, were simply not high enough. He merely put off taking the entrance exams indefinitely.

Unfortunately for him, Yeats's time in Howth (which also happened to be the birthplace of his future beloved, Maud Gonne) was as limited as his time at Erasmus. In 1883, he moved with his family to a brick building at 10 Ashfield Terrace (now ❺ **418 Harold's Cross Road**) in the suburb of Terenure. It was clearly outside of respectable Dublin, and Yeats did not enjoy his time there. His only escape was through education.

Without the scores to get into Trinity, Yeats's options were severely limited. In May 1884, he ended up at the ❻ **Dublin Metropolitan School of Art** (now called the National College of Art and Design and located on Thomas Street), one of the least expensive options for

The "cloakroom" at Erasmus High School was vast enough that Yeats could play chess while his teacher taught math lessons.

the financially challenged Yeats family. His father taught at the school, and his sisters attended it as well.

Although tremendously bored by the curriculum, Yeats made a number of interesting friends there, including George Russell, whose energies and enthusiasm for

John Butler Yeats painted this portrait of AE.

the Wicklow hills talking animatedly, Russell about the visions he had while painting and Yeats about his future writing projects; he is said to have worked out most of his play *The Shadowy Waters* while walking Leinster Road with Russell. Russell soon became known as AE due to a printer's error in rendering "Aeon," a Gnostic term that Russell intended to use as his pen name.

Although Yeats and AE eventually went their separate ways, AE was an important figure in the Irish Literary Revival. His poetry is not widely read today, but his collections of mystically inspired poems had great impact on the Dublin cultural scene at the time and brought him many admirers. In turn, he served as a mentor to a number of younger Irish poets and was a friend of George Moore, scenery artist for the Irish Literary Theatre, and editor of *The Irish Homestead*, the magazine of the Irish Agricultural Organization Society.

J. M. Synge's Childhood

Another writer who spent his childhood south of the Liffey also had a central role in the Irish Literary Revival. John Millington Synge was born on April 16, 1871, in nearby Rathfarnham, where his family lived at ❼ **2 Newtown Villas.** Shortly after Synge was born, his father died of smallpox and the Synges moved. Although tormented by the fears of hell and sin instilled in him by his zealous mother, Synge had a mostly happy childhood roaming the Wicklow hills before attending Trinity College and studying music in Europe.

Sean O'Casey's Neighborhood

Whereas Synge traveled to the far west of Ireland to find a community at the edge of existence, Sean

mysticism matched Yeats's. Yeats dedicated his 1889 collection of poetry, *Crossways*, to Russell and even based the character Michael Robartes in his short story "Rosa Alchemica" on him. Yeats describes Robartes as having "wild red hair, fierce eyes, sensitive, tremulous lips and rough clothes [that] made him look . . . something between a debauchee, a saint, and a peasant."

Russell lived near the Yeats family in Terenure, and the two young men would walk along Leinster Road toward

O'Casey grew up among people fighting daily for survival. In the early twentieth century, the area north of the Liffey beyond what is now O'Connell Street was a Dublin slum. It was in that area, at ❽ **Upper Dorset Street,** on March 30, 1880, that O' Casey was born. His family belonged to the social class then known as "shabby genteel." This meant that, although Protestant and educated, the O'Caseys struggled to make ends meet and relied on the labor of their children to keep food on the table. O'Casey's father died when Sean was six, leaving his mother with six mouths to feed. As their fortunes declined, the family moved from house to house throughout Dublin.

The once glorious Mountjoy Square was a squalid tenement outpost while Sean O'Casey lived there but is being freshened by urban renewal.

John Casey, as he was known before he took on the more Irish name of Sean O'Casey, could not attend school because of trouble with his eyes. He taught himself to read and write when he was fourteen.

As an adult, O'Casey lived in an apartment at ❾ **35 Mountjoy Square** while working on *The Shadow of a Gunman*. The square was developed between 1792 and 1818 by Luke Gardiner, the Viscount of Mountjoy; once elegant, it was abandoned and left to ruin. (It is now restored.) Poverty, typhoid, tuberculosis, and political strife marked much of O'Casey's life there. In fact, the events of *The Shadow of a Gunman* were taken from his experiences in the apartment building.

Before his Abbey Theatre successes gave him enough income to write full-time, O'Casey worked at the Dublin docks and around north Dublin as a "casual worker," or day laborer, where he became involved with Jim Larkin and the Irish Transport and General Workers' Union. After learning Gaelic, he participated in the Gaelic League, the Irish Republican Brotherhood, and the Irish Citizen Army, which fought (without O' Casey) under James Connolly in the 1916 Easter Rising.

The Irish Theater: Windows to Heaven, Floor of Earth

Prior to that rainy afternoon in the west of Ireland when Lady Gregory sat with Yeats over tea and charted the course of Irish drama, there were only three theaters of

Sean O'Casey in the 1930s.

rowdy, quick-tempered brute or the happy-go-lucky buffoon. In either case, the character was often drunk and illiterate.

Yeats, Lady Gregory, and Edward Martyn sought to overcome this portrayal of the Irish. In the letter sent out from Lady Gregory's Coole Park estate, the three declared their intention to "show that Ireland is not the home of buffoonery and of easy sentiment, as it has been represented, but the home of an ancient idealism."

Part of the problem was the audience. Used to the melodramas and comic sketches brought in by English companies, Dublin theatergoers had little experience with literary drama dealing with Irish content. George Moore even counseled Yeats and Martyn to produce their plays in London because their good qualities would be wasted on the Dubliners, later writing, "If the plays were going to be acted in London it would be a different thing, but to ally myself to such folly as the bringing of literature to Ireland!"

As it turned out, there would be numerous hurdles to surmount. The fledgling project did not have enough money to rent an established theater, for instance, and a city statute made it illegal to present plays for profit in any other hall. Upon discovering this, Lady Gregory mobilized her connections and was able to get an amendment passed allowing the use of the ❿ **Antient Concert Rooms**, at **42 Pearse Street** (formerly Great Brunswick).

note in Dublin: the Gaiety, the Royal, and the Queen's. They featured plays written by English writers, played by English actors, for an English audience. If an Irish character appeared in the plays, it was as caricature: the

The two plays offered on May 8, 1899, were Martyn's *The Heather Field* and Yeats's *The Countess Cathleen*. Prior to the opening curtain of the first play, a prologue written by the poet Lionel Johnson was presented to the audience. The final stanza invited the audience in:

> Come, then, and keep with us an Irish feast,
> Wherein the Lord of Light and Song is priest;
> Now, at this opening of gentle May,
> Watch warring passions at their storm and play;
> Wrought with the flaming ecstasy of art,
> Sprung from the dreaming of an Irish heart.

In many ways, this first performance was a microcosm of the Irish theater movement, displaying many of its recurring themes: the financial and political support needed for artistic freedom, the reactions and interactions with the audience, and the often contradictory visions of what constitutes "nationalist" drama. As would happen repeatedly, "warring passions" stormed around the plays put on by Yeats and Lady Gregory.

The Countess Cathleen recounts the story of an Irish woman who sells her soul to the devil to save her neighbors from the ravages of the Famine. Students from University College, whom the theater critic Joseph Holloway characterized as "twenty brainless, beardless youths," "coughed, hissed, stamped their feet and generally disrupted the show." In the days following the performance, these same students wrote a letter of protest to the newspapers. (One University College student who declined to sign the letter was James Joyce, who enjoyed the performance and refused to contribute to the literary censorship that would eventually drive him into exile.)

At stake was the central issue of the portrayal of the Irish. Looking to claim the Irish Literary Theatre for nationalist purposes, these students and a few other Dubliners were taken aback by Yeats's suggestion that an Irish woman would sell her soul to the devil, even for a noble purpose.

An Irish Play, in Irish, for an Irish Audience

The 1900 season included English actors presenting a play by Alice Milligan, along with Martyn's *Maeve* and a George Moore rewrite of a Martyn play, *The Bending of the Bough*. But the real excitement came on October 21, 1901, when the Irish Literary Theatre presented

Actor William Fay and his brother Frank were instrumental in creating an Irish theatrical style and bringing in audiences to the Abbey Theatre.

115

Douglas Hyde's play in Gaelic, *Casadh an tSugan*, at the ⑪ **Gaiety Theatre.**

This play, the first to be produced in the Irish language in a major theater, was based on Yeats's story of Red Hanrahan, "The Twisting of the Rope." It was presented along with *Diarmuid and Grania,* the result of an uneasy collaboration between George Moore and Yeats, in a theater that sat a thousand patrons. The Irish theater movement had come a long way since that intimate conversation between two friends in the west of Ireland just a few years before.

Although many in the audience could not follow the play in Irish, Douglas Hyde, who played the lead character, apparently had such stage presence that it mattered little. He played an itinerant poet and music maker with such a wonderful swagger that few could believe this was the same dignified, occasionally stiff academic who led the Gaelic League. Lady Gregory describes the effect:

This time we also produced Casad-an-Sugan . . . *by the founder of the Gaelic League, Dr. Douglas Hyde. He himself acted the chief part in it and*

Mad for Maud

When Yeats met Maud Gonne in London in 1889, it was a life-changing event. Her beauty struck him first: "That day she seemed a classical impersonation of the Spring, the Virgillian commendation 'She walks like a goddess' made for her alone. Her complexion was luminous, like that of apple-blossom through which the light falls."

He later proposed to her not once or twice but repeatedly. She denied him every time, claiming that a spiritual union with him was far superior to a physical one. He also came very close to marrying her daughter Iseult in 1916, but in the end she too turned him down.

In any case, the love between Yeats and Gonne remained a mystical one. Gonne abhorred physical passion, although she had a number of affairs, gave birth to two children, and married a war hero, John McBride, in 1903. She preferred to remain Yeats's muse, justifying his torment by the quality of the poetry he wrote about her. She described them as having a "celestial marriage," linked by their souls and imaginations rather than by mere physical connection.

According to popular interpretations of their letters, they did cross the line once, in December 1908. Unfortunately for Yeats, that one night was not enough to satisfy him or to sway her, and they remained purely platonic after that.

Maud Gonne, Yeats's muse, was known throughout Ireland for her beauty.

even to those who had no Irish, the performance was a delight, it was played with so much gaiety, ease and charm. It was the first time a play written in Irish had ever been seen in a Dublin theatre.

Although the Irish Literary Theatre came to the end of its original three-year mandate in 1901, the idea of an Irish national theater was kept alive. The most important step may have been the founding of the Irish National Dramatic Company in 1902 by William and Frank Fay. These two brothers recognized the need for Irish actors to be trained in speaking Irish parts. They realized that an Irish theater that relied on English actors was simply not sufficient.

The Fays had first come into contact with the Irish Literary Revival through AE, who introduced them to Yeats. In April 1902, they collaborated with Yeats and Lady Gregory to produce AE's *Deirdre* and Yeats and Lady Gregory's *Cathleen Ni Houlihan* at ⑫ **St. Teresa's Total Abstinence Hall** on Clarendon Street. With the tall and strikingly beautiful Maud Gonne in the title role, *Cathleen Ni Houlihan* struck the right patriotic note, and the audience of three hundred responded with emotion, applause, and nationalist songs. The play cemented Maud Gonne's reputation; her dramatic entrance down the center aisle was long remembered by many. The Fay brothers, for their part, would go on to help form the Irish National Theatre Society, which produced plays put on with the Irish National Dramatic Company, and become fixtures at the Abbey Theatre.

The production created the momentum for the formation of the Irish National Theatre Society in 1902 with Yeats as president and AE as vice president. That season included several plays by Yeats, one by Padraic Colum, and the theatrical debut of Lady

Gregory with *Twenty-Five*. The society also produced J. M. Synge's first play, *In the Shadow of the Glen*, at ⑬ **Molesworth Hall** on October 8, 1903; his *Riders to the Sea* followed in 1904.

The Abbey Theatre: A Home for Controversy

Riding on the success of *Cathleen Ni Houlihan,* the Irish National Theatre Society was further blessed in

This theater was known by a series of names, including the Theatre Royal, the Hibernian, the Princess Theatre of Varieties, and the Mechanics Institute, before becoming the Abbey Theatre in 1904.

1904 when Annie Horniman, the daughter of an English tea merchant, decided to use part of her inheritance to give Yeats a theater where he could fulfill his mission of bringing Irish art into public view.

Horniman bought and had renovated an old theater called the Mechanics Institute, as well as the adjoining building, which had been a morgue. (The morgue coughed up part of a human skeleton during the renovation, and the presence of ghosts was occasionally felt.) The society would eventually make this one of the most famous theaters in the world: the ⓮ **Abbey Theatre** on **Lower Abbey Street**.

The Abbey was constructed to give a feeling of intimacy. It had 562 seats, a workable stage with wings, a grand foyer, and an entrance boasting stained-glass windows.

The actors relaxed and prepared in the downstairs greenroom. On opening nights it was often filled with an enormous barm brack, or fruitcake, specially made for Lady Gregory in Gort and hauled to Dublin by train. This cake was legendary at the Abbey and was the object of both gratitude and scorn: One of the actors, Maire Ni Shiubhlaigh, described it as

a huge cart-wheel of a fruit cake, filled with the richest ingredients, made specially by her own bakers at Gort for the casts of any of her new plays. It was a huge affair of several pounds weight and usually took two to carry in. It must have been two feet in circumference, and fully eight inches in depth.

Some of the actors appreciated the solid meal afforded by this enormous cake, while others found it an easy target for satire. Willie Fay called it "the father and mother of a brack."

Some of Ireland's finest shows were performed (and fiercest battles waged) in this theater.

Queen Maeve has served as a symbol of the Abbey Theatre for more than a hundred years.

The *Playboy* Riots

During the fall of 1906, J. M. Synge was hard at work on another play based on a tale he had heard on the Aran Islands. The story—of a man named Christy Mahon, who kills his father in retribution for a life of misery, escapes, and is welcomed by a community in bleak western Ireland—provided Synge with the framework; additional material from County Mayo, where he set the play, filled out the rest of the narrative.

The play's harsh and often coarse language shocked many in the company. Lady Gregory suggested some initial revisions, to which Synge consented, but the cast remained reluctant to stage the show. Synge was concerned enough to pen a program note explaining the play's origins and meanings:

> In writing "The Playboy of the Western World," as in my other plays, I have used one or two words only that I have not heard among the country people of Ireland, or spoken in my own nursery before I could read the newspapers. A certain number of the phrases I employ I have heard also from herds and fishermen along the coast from Kerry to Mayo, or from beggar-women and ballad-singers nearer Dublin; and I am glad to acknowledge how much I owe to the folk imagination of these fine people. Anyone who has lived in real intimacy with the Irish peasantry will know that the wildest sayings and ideas in this play are tame indeed, compared with the fancies one may hear in any little hillside cabin in Geesala, or Carraroe, or Dingle Bay.

The Abbey Theatre formally opened its doors on December 27, 1904, with *Cathleen Ni Houlihan*, Yeats's *On Baile's Strand*, and a new comedy written by Lady Gregory to fill out the evening, *Spreading the News*. On the second night, Synge's controversial play about a woman who leaves her husband for a tramp, *In the Shadow of the Glen*, replaced Lady Gregory's play. It provoked criticism for its portrayal of a woman who leaves her marriage for life with a solitary traveler. Irish women did not do those sorts of things, the audiences felt (although the plot came from a story told to Synge on Inis Meáin).

On January 26, 1907, the theater opened to a respectable but not full house. The audience enjoyed Synge's short tragedy *Riders to the Sea* and sat through the opening act of *Playboy* without incident. Lady Gregory sent a telegram to Yeats, who was lecturing that night in Aberdeen, Scotland: "Play great success."

As the play continued, however, the language began to elicit more and more reaction from the audience. By the time the supposedly murdered father returned to claim his son, some in the audience were nearly hysterical with shock and dismay. When the son declared, "It's Pegeen Mike [the pub owner's daughter] I'm seeking only, and what'd I care if you brought me a drift of chosen females, standing in their shifts itself, maybe, from this place to the Eastern World?" the audience brought the play to a standstill with boos, hisses, and shouts, outraged at the use of the word *shift* (an indelicate word for a woman's underwear). Shortly afterward, another telegram was dispatched to Yeats: "Audience broke up in disorder at the word 'shift.' "

Synge wrote to his future fiancée, Molly Allgood, that they had been made famous: "It is better to have the row we had last night, than to have your play fizzling out in halfhearted applause. Now we'll be talked about. We're an event in the history of the Irish stage."

The next performance was disrupted again by protesters, whose din made much of the play unintelligible. The following night Lady Gregory recruited a nephew and his friends from Trinity College, who tried to shush the demonstrators when their boos began; they, in turn, shouted louder. One man finally rushed the stage, only to be dragged off by the actor playing Christy Mahon's father and by Synge himself. Although the play continued, with the dialogue often drowned out by shouting, tempers flared in street fights near the Trinity College gates later in the evening.

The next night, fifty police were in the hall and the place was full. There were shouts and hisses but not the chaos of the night before. By Thursday night, five nights after the play's debut, the police numbered two hundred, and the play was given a reasonable hearing for the first time. *Playboy* finished its run with a moderated debate on the play hosted by the Abbey. A week later, the theater was again quiet and working on a new production, Lady Gregory's *Jackdaw*.

The Abbey nurtured the talent of another young writer: Sean O'Casey's first play, *The Shadow of a Gunman*, debuted on April 12, 1923, to packed houses. His second play at the Abbey, *Juno and the Paycock*, helped save the theater from bankruptcy in 1924.

Although *Juno's* success was based on its humor, the play was critical of the Dublin slums and the type of shiftless, opportunistic character seen by O'Casey as endemic there. The play's main character, known as "the Paycock," is unable to provide for his family in the hardscrabble world of the Dublin tenements.

At heart, however, the Paycock was a character Dublin could recognize and acknowledge as part of its makeup. Not so with Rosie from O'Casey's next play, *The Plough and the Stars*. Rosie is a prostitute, and her appearance in a play set during the 1916 rising, on the same stage as the tricolor Irish flag, was too much for the nationalistic audience to handle; they rioted when the play was put on in February 1926. As with Synge's *Playboy*, the major problems came not on the first night but later in the run. After hisses and catcalls during the first act on the fourth night, a chorus of shouting and heckling broke out in Act II. During Act III, some audience members, mostly women, rushed the stage and attacked the actors, who fought back. One man was punched so hard by the actor Barry Fitzgerald that he went flying back into the audience.

This time, however, the Abbey was better prepared. Again, Yeats called in the police, happily noting that "this time it would be their own police," and not the British police. Although the presence of the uniformed guard of the Irish Republic kept some of the troublemakers in check, the audience still made enough noise to drown out the actors. The curtain was dropped, and the house lights went on to calm everyone.

Yeats waited, seething, behind the curtain until he heard a lull. Suddenly appearing onstage, he lectured

Arrested in America: The Abbey on Tour

When Lady Gregory and Yeats conspired together at Doorus House on that rainy afternoon in 1897, their dreams of an Irish theater included the possibility of a tour to what Lady Gregory called "the greater Ireland beyond the Atlantic." In 1911, that dream came true. The theater managers of Liebler & Company offered the Abbey company a contract to go to America with a number of plays, including *The Playboy of the Western World*. Lady Gregory took control of the trip and left Ireland aboard the *Cymric* on September 20, 1911, for a five-month, thirty-one-city tour.

They landed first in Boston, where Yeats had already given a few lectures to large, receptive audiences. Lady Gregory immediately felt at home there: "Boston is a very friendly place. There are so many Irish there that I had been told at home there is a part of it called Galway, and I met many old friends." Providence, Rhode Island, proved to be just as welcoming, although Lady Gregory was called before the police commissioner to verify that there was nothing scandalous in the plays.

The company arrived in New York on November 18. Lady Gregory stayed at the Algonquin Hotel, where Dorothy Parker and her circle would soon hold court in the Rose Room. Nine days later, the company gave its first production of *Playboy* in New York. Just as in Dublin, shouts and whistles filled the theater. The police came in but made no arrests. Backstage, Lady Gregory told the actors to continue playing but not to strain their voices. Once they finished the play, they decided to do the whole thing again because nobody had been heard. This time, the audience was quiet all the way through.

The next night Lady Gregory invited her friend Franklin Roosevelt, who took a bow with her from his box. The remaining nights' audiences were respectful. For her part, Gregory understood that it was the recent Irish immigrants who caused the trouble. When told that Americans shouldn't be held responsible, she quipped, "No, our countrymen took care to make that clear by throwing our national potato. If you had attacked us, you would have thrown pumpkins."

The performances in New York were also notable for their effect on one particular audience member. The playwright Eugene O'Neill was struck by the Abbey repertoire, particularly *Riders to the Sea*, and later declared that the performance at the Odeon "was what first opened my eyes to the existence of a real theatre."

Philadelphia proved to be an adventure as well. The cast was arrested on January 18, just before the evening performance, on warrants forbidding "immoral or indecent plays." The theater manager stepped in and prevented the warrants from being served right away, and that night *Playboy* played to a completely full house—even Lady Gregory couldn't find a seat.

The next morning the entire cast was brought to a magistrate's court, and a trial was scheduled for that afternoon. The trial was under way when American lawyer and friend of many in the Revival John Quinn arrived to take control of the proceedings. As Quinn questioned the opposing witnesses, they all lost credibility, one of them declaring that "a theatre is no place for a sense of humour." The group was allowed to continue its American tour, traveling as far west as Chicago, and the charges were eventually dropped.

Edmund Dulac's interpretation of the real dynamics of the Abbey Theatre.

the audience: "You have disgraced yourselves again. Is this to be an ever-recurring celebration of the arrival of Irish genius? Dublin has again rocked the cradle of a reputation. From such a theatre as this went forth the fame of Synge. Equally, the fame of O'Casey is born here tonight. This is his apotheosis." *Apotheosis*, as the playwright in question had to look up in his dictionary, means "an exaltation to divine rank or stature." Public spectacle had again made the reputation of a deeply private writer.

Today's Abbey:
A Hundred Years On and Ready to Move

The Abbey Theatre has remained a visible, if not always viable, institution in Dublin. The first major theater to be subsidized by the state (thanks in large part to the efforts of Senator W. B. Yeats and Lady Gregory), the Abbey has continued to offer a mix of plays, from the poetic and abstract to the perenially popular, but the original theater no longer stands.

After the evening performance of O'Casey's *The Plough and the Stars* on July 17, 1951, the Abbey Theatre as Yeats and Gregory knew it burned to the ground. Undaunted, the company performed the play again the next night in what was left of the adjoining Peacock Theatre, with whatever props and scenery they could pick from the ashes.

After that makeshift performance, however, the Irish National Theatre had to perform in the (now demolished) ⓖ Queen's Theatre

for fifteen years until the Abbey could be replaced. Finally, on July 18, 1966, the current Abbey opened its doors. The new building, a concrete-block structure with little charm, seats 628, with an additional 157 in the Peacock Theatre.

However impressive its history or recent productions, the Abbey continues to have an uncertain future. In December 2005, the Irish minister for arts announced plans to move the theater to a new location at George's Dock in the Dublin Docklands area. The new location would allow the creation of a modern, state-of-the-art theater with ample seating and modern equipment, as well as rehearsal spaces for both the Peacock Theatre and the Abbey.

The Easter Rising

Perhaps only in Ireland would a revolution such as the Easter Rising, a brief and ill-fated effort to overthrow

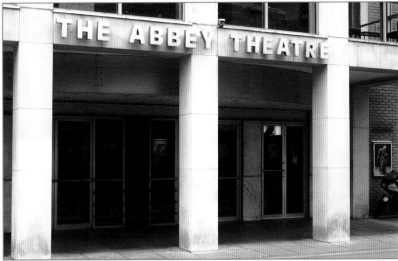

This architecturally uninspired building housed the Abbey Theatre for more than forty years.

British rule, be fought by so many writers. Padraig Pearse and Thomas MacDonagh were both poets, and MacDonagh, Joseph Plunkett, Willie Pearse, and Padraic O'Connor were involved in Edward Martyn's Hardwicke Street Theatre. These were not hardened soldiers or gun-happy mercenaries.

POBLACHT NA H EIREANN.

THE PROVISIONAL GOVERNMENT

OF THE

IRISH REPUBLIC

TO THE PEOPLE OF IRELAND.

IRISHMEN AND IRISHWOMEN : In the name of God and of the dead generations from which she receives her old tradition of nationhood, Ireland, through us, summons her children to her flag and strikes for her freedom.

Having organised and trained her manhood through her secret revolutionary organisation, the Irish Republican Brotherhood, and through her open military organisations, the Irish Volunteers and the Irish Citizen Army, having patiently perfected her discipline, having resolutely waited for the right moment to reveal itself, she now seizes that moment, and, supported by her exiled children in America and by gallant allies in Europe, but relying in the first on her own strength, she strikes in full confidence of victory.

We declare the right of the people of Ireland to the ownership of Ireland, and to the unfettered control of Irish destinies, to be sovereign and indefeasible. The long usurpation of that right by a foreign people and government has not extinguished the right, nor can it ever be extinguished except by the destruction of the Irish people. In every generation the Irish people have asserted their right to national freedom and sovereignty; six times during the past three hundred years they have asserted it in arms. Standing on that fundamental right and again asserting it in arms in the face of the world, we hereby proclaim the Irish Republic as a Sovereign Independent State, and we pledge our lives and the lives of our comrades-in-arms to the cause of its freedom, of its welfare, and of its exaltation among the nations.

The Irish Republic is entitled to, and hereby claims, the allegiance of every Irishman and Irishwoman. The Republic guarantees religious and civil liberty, equal rights and equal opportunities to all its citizens, and declares its resolve to pursue the happiness and prosperity of the whole nation and of all its parts, cherishing all the children of the nation equally, and oblivious of the differences carefully fostered by an alien government, which have divided a minority from the majority in the past.

Until our arms have brought the opportune moment for the establishment of a permanent National Government, representative of the whole people of Ireland and elected by the suffrages of all her men and women, the Provisional Government, hereby constituted, will administer the civil and military affairs of the Republic in trust for the people.

We place the cause of the Irish Republic under the protection of the Most High God, Whose blessing we invoke upon our arms, and we pray that no one who serves that cause will dishonour it by cowardice, inhumanity, or rapine. In this supreme hour the Irish nation must, by its valour and discipline and by the readiness of its children to sacrifice themselves for the common good, prove itself worthy of the august destiny to which it is called.

Signed on Behalf of the Provisional Government,

THOMAS J. CLARKE,
SEAN Mac DIARMADA, THOMAS MacDONAGH,
P. H. PEARSE, EAMONN CEANNT,
JAMES CONNOLLY. JOSEPH PLUNKETT.

Constance Markievicz read this proclamation from the steps of Liberty Hall, while Padraig Pearse read it at the General Post Office.

What they were was a motley collection of a few hundred men and women from a variety of secret societies and paramilitary groups willing to take on the British Empire. The original plan was to seize strategic buildings throughout Dublin. Many of the men wore the uniforms of the Irish Citizen Army, a group formed by labor leader James Connolly in 1913 to protect Dublin dockworkers during a lockout. Others were from a group called the Irish Volunteers. Still others were drawn from a secret society called the Irish Republican Brotherhood, which was dedicated to armed insurgence against British rule in Ireland. Formed in 1858, the IRB was occasionally known as the Fenians.

When these groups marched up to the ⑯ **General Post Office** on April 24, 1916, it was the last gasp of a plan that originally had much potential. The leaders of the rebellion had been planning for many months in great secrecy. A man named Roger Casement had been sent to procure arms from the Germans, who were only too happy to have the Irish provide another distraction for the English during World War I. Unfortunately for the Germans and the Irish, the German ship the *Aud*, carrying arms for the rebels, was intercepted off the coast of Ireland, and the cache had to be scuttled. Casement was captured, and the British authorities began to sniff out the plan. One of the leaders, Eoin MacNeill, called off all revolutionary activities planned for Easter Sunday.

The military council of the IRB overruled MacNeill the next day, however, and Constance Markievicz read the Proclamation of the Irish Republic on the steps of Liberty Hall, the trade union headquarters, before the groups marched off to various positions around the city. Once inside the post office, Padraig Pearse read the proclamation to the Dublin public. With garrisons in the Royal College of Surgeons on St. Stephen's Green, at Boland's Mill, and at other sites scattered around the city a few unsuccessful attacks were made on British targets, such as ⑰ Dublin Castle.

Mostly, though, the rebels just dug in and waited for the inevitable counterattack, which came over the next few days. Much of the area around the post office and the other garrisons was heavily shelled by the British gunboat *Helga* moored in the River Liffey. With the post office burning and the few remaining resisters surrounded, Pearse formally surrendered on Saturday morning. It was all over.

After a series of brief trials, fifteen rebel leaders were sentenced to death by firing squad. The prolonged executions (it took nine days for the British to shoot everyone) turned popular opinion against the British. The rebels, who had marched off to jail dodging curses and rotten fruit thrown at them by hostile onlookers, became martyrs upon their deaths. By the time the remaining prisoners were released, many Irish viewed them as true heroes. It would not be long before the Irish rebelled again, more successfully, in 1919.

Private Experience, Public Art: A Response to the Easter Rising

It is fitting that the best-known response to the Easter Rising came from a poet. Yeats wrote "Easter, 1916" in the months after the uprising; the first sixteen lines were excerpted and published in the *Irish Commonwealth* in March 1919, and the poem appeared in its entirety in 1920 in the *New Statesman*. In this poem, Yeats treads a fine line between admiration and revulsion, finally granting a begrudging respect to the men and women involved.

At first he describes them as mere figures traversing a gray Dublin world where nothing is done and only "polite meaningless words" are exchanged. He describes players in the rebellion; some portraits flatter, such as his description of Pearse and MacDonagh, while others are less complimentary. He admits to thinking of one character (John McBride, the man who married Maud Gonne) as a "drunken, vainglorious lout."

Their personal sacrifices in the uprising have a transformative power, however, and by the end of the poem all these men and women, no matter their earlier faults and foibles, have become heroes. Even if Yeats is still unsure what they have accomplished or whether their sacrifices were heroic, he has decided to celebrate them:

After intense shelling during the Easter Rising, much of downtown Dublin was destroyed.

I write it out in a verse—
MacDonagh and MacBride
And Connolly and Pearse
Now and in time to be,
Wherever green is worn,
Are changed, changed utterly:
A terrible beauty is born.

In the Wings: The Private Spheres of Dublin

The Irish Literary Revival also took place in clubs and private homes, in far less sensational situations than the Easter Rising or the theater riots. Revival participants worked more quietly in printing houses and public offices. Many of the smaller-scale activities were centered across the River Liffey in a small section of Dublin bordered by Ely Place and St. Stephen's Green on the southern edge, Grafton Street on the west, Trinity College on the north, and Merrion Square on the east.

Perhaps the most interesting education for writers such as Yeats and AE occurred not at any of the educational institutions in the city but at ⓮ **8 Ely Place,** where the Dublin Theosophical Society met. As Yeats describes it, it was a place where young men and women could focus on more ethereal subjects: "The one house where nobody thought or talked politics was a house in Ely Place, where a number of young men lived together, and, for want of a better name, were called Theosophists." The Dublin Theosophical Society was a group of young thinkers willing to take on a wide variety of nontraditional subjects, including mysticism, Hinduism, Buddhism, spirituality, and occultism. The house, which still stands, is a fine example of the city's well-maintained Georgian mansions.

A little farther down Ely Place was where George Moore lived from 1901 to 1910. When Moore returned to his native Ireland from England to escape the jingoism connected with the Boer Wars and to take part in the Irish Literary Revival, he looked for just the right type of home for a cultured gentleman. His friend AE found the perfect spot for him, and Moore took the

To irritate his neighbors, George Moore painted his door "Fenian green" when the neighborhood regulations stipulated that it must be white. (It has since been changed.)

rooms at ⓳ **4 Ely Place** in the spring of 1901. It was a nice place, not overly ostentatious but quite spacious, with a large yard and proximity to the heart of Dublin's social network. Quickly establishing himself as a neighborhood eccentric, Moore chose to paint his front door "Fenian green" in spite of neighborhood regulations limiting door color to white. When confronted by the neighborhood supervisor, he claimed, as an art expert, that the green door was a necessary component of his decorating scheme.

Thus began a war between Moore and his neighbors that dragged on for years. It was exacerbated when he produced Douglas Hyde's play *The Tinker and the Fairy* on May 19, 1902, in his backyard, much to the chagrin of his Unionist, Protestant neighbors, who heckled from their upper windows. Some of the neighboring women took a copy of his novel *Esther Waters* and tore it up, then put the pieces in his mailbox with a note saying "too filthy to keep in the house." In retribution for such insults, Moore would stroll out in the middle of the night and rattle his walking stick along the iron fence in front of his neighbors' houses. The loud noise set dogs to barking wildly; Moore ambled peacefully into the night.

When he wasn't at war with his neighbors, Moore was quite the man about town. Oliver St. John Gogarty, a neighbor on Ely Place, described him this way:

A figure with hair silver as a dandelion in summer, pink porcelain face, sloping shoulders and peg-topped trousers in a suit of navy blue, came strolling down Ely Place from its garden end . . . he strolled

This cartoon pokes fun at two of Dublin's cultural icons, Yeats and AE. They have set out to meet each other, but because Yeats has his head in the clouds and AE is staring at the ground, they pass each other.

leisurely, as became a novelist, a personage and a man of independent means.

When he wasn't rabble-rousing with nationalist activities or strolling through nearby St. Stephen's Green, Moore was reading at the National Library or hosting evening literary gatherings at his house. These gatherings allowed the Dublin intelligentsia to air ideas, compare theories, and posture endlessly.

A rising young star of these evenings, Oliver St. John Gogarty lived just down the street at ❷⓿ **15 Ely Place.** A surgeon, poet, and wit, Gogarty is perhaps best known for the character he inspired in James Joyce's *Ulysses*, Buck Mulligan, but he had ties to the Revival as well. He made his name, ironically, with an anonymously published poem, "Ode of Welcome." The acrostic poem (the letters at the beginning of each line spell out "The Whores Will Be Busy") sold out in a matter of hours, and it didn't take long for cultural figures such as Yeats and Moore to hunt down its author. They then quickly introduced him into their literary evenings, where his wit and intelligent conversation were much admired.

Merrion Square: Home of the Statesman

After living in London for many years and returning to Ireland only during the summers, Yeats decided to buy a house in Dublin. His wife, George, picked out a house at ❷❶ **82 Merrion Square,** just two doors down from AE at 84. (Yeats also lived for a brief time at 52 Merrion Square.)

It was while Yeats lived here that he was elected to the Irish Free State Senate and received the Nobel Prize. As Yeats himself recognized, it was a fitting home for the public figure he had become: "It puts back my family into some kind of dignity & gives my children a stately home, & and myself a background for old age."

As biographer R. F. Foster describes, the house was decorated in the Yeatses' distinct style:

> *Ricketts watercolours of stage-sets hung in the hall. George introduced some Omega Workshop precepts into the Georgian rooms: there was painted furniture, blue and orange hangings, tall candles everywhere. A cage of canaries took up residence in the study window, woodcuts were grouped on the walls, carved tables were piled with books. A bedroom ceiling was painted blue with gold stars.*

Merrion Square was laid out between 1762 and 1764 and had long been a respectable address. Oscar Wilde was born on one corner, AE lived there, and Lady Gregory's mother moved there after her husband died. Today the square retains many of the impressive Georgian houses that made this such a perfect location for Yeats.

The Yeatses particularly liked the open rooms and large windows of their abode—although during the civil war, bullets occasionally came flying in through those windows. One buried itself in the nursery wall above George, spraying plaster down on her and their daughter Anne, while another ended up in the bedroom wall. The threat of violence to the senator of the young Irish Free State sent the household's maid packing for home

What to Do When You Win the Nobel Prize

On the evening of November 14, 1923, Yeats received a phone call from the editor of the *Irish Times*, Bertie Smyllie. According to Smyllie, news of Yeats's having won the Nobel Prize in Literature had just come over the wire. Yeats's reaction, according to his son, was to ask, "How much is it? How much?" Later, Yeats and his wife went down to the kitchen and, because they had no champagne in the house, cooked up sausages for a celebration.

in Galway. But once the Troubles settled down, the Yeatses enjoyed their Dublin house and Yeats became, once again, an important figure in Dublin's social scene.

In the summer of 1923, 82 Merrion Square became the new home of Cuala Press, the artistic publishing house run by Yeats's two sisters. Lily Yeats became very sick that summer, and Lolly moved the business into the ground-floor rooms at 82 Merrion Square. Yeats's wife, George, joined the venture and helped keep it going for years.

When Yeats's term as a senator ended in 1928, so did his yearly stipend of 360 pounds, and the Yeatses decided to move from their stately house on Merrion Square to a farmhouse in Rathfarnham, the town where J. M. Synge was born. From their house they could see the Wicklow Mountains, and Yeats could sit and enjoy his garden.

Death of a Playboy

Synge also returned to this area, when he was ill with Hodgkin's disease. He was brought to ㉒ **Elpis Private Hospital, 19–20 Lower Mount Street,** where, if he could have raised himself in bed, he would have seen the Wicklow hills. He penned this poem shortly before his death in 1909:

> *On an Anniversary*
> *After reading the dates in a book of lyrics*

Dun Emer Industries and Cuala Press

During the early twentieth century, the Arts and Crafts movement in Ireland encouraged women to develop marketable artistic skills that would provide income for them and their families. Classes were offered in convents and in the houses of the landed gentry. This movement resulted in three studios where women could work: the Irish Decorative Arts Association, founded by Mina Robinson and Elta Lowry to do needlework and decorative touches on wooden furniture; An Tur Gloine (Tower of Glass), started by Sarah Purser (who did the stained-glass windows for the Abbey Theatre); and Dun Emer Industries, founded by Evelyn Gleeson and Lily and Lolly Yeats. Dun Emer focused on weaving and tapestry until Lolly learned how to work a printing press. Then it began crafting hand-printed products under the occasional "guidance" of their brother Willie, who served as literary adviser to the press. These ventures were noteworthy in that nearly all the employees were women, at a time when there were not many options available to them.

In 1908, the Yeats sisters left Dun Emer to start their own printing shop, Cuala Press, first out of a cottage in the Dublin suburb of Churchtown, and then from Yeats's house on Merrion Square. They specialized in beautifully crafted books, Christmas cards, and broadsides. They printed draft versions of much of their brother William's poetry, frequently using illustrations painted by their brother Jack. The press faded into obscurity until revived in 1970 by Anne Yeats, the poet's daughter.

Yeats's sisters, Lily and Lolly, worked together (later with his wife, George) to produce seventy titles.

Hugh Lane Gallery

Although Lady Gregory's nephew, Hugh Lane, was born in County Cork, he was brought up in England. It was through his frequent visits to Coole Park that he established a connection with Ireland and with the major figures of the Irish Literary Revival. After an early career restoring paintings, Lane became one of London's most successful art dealers.

Lane was convinced that Dublin needed a modern art museum with a core collection of national and international pieces, and he purchased many of those pieces himself. His choice for a site was the Halfpenny Bridge in Dublin, where he envisioned a modern building spanning the river. Unfortunately, Lane met with significant resistance from Dublin city officials and, in a fit of pique, he decided to give his entire collection to London instead.

He later recanted, however, and signed a codicil to his will stating that upon his death his collection should go to Dublin. Unfortunately, the codicil was not witnessed, so after Lane died aboard the *Lusitania* in 1915, the paintings went to the National Gallery of London. After years of impassioned campaigning by Lady Gregory and others, the British and Irish governments reached a sharing agreement in 1959, making Lane's collection the only major collection in the world that regularly commutes between two cities. Parts of the collection are rotated every six months between the ㉓ **Hugh Lane Gallery** in Dublin and the Tate Gallery in London.

The gallery in Dublin now houses almost two thousand works of art by Manet, Monet, Degas, Renoir, and Ireland's own Jack Yeats. The gallery is in Charlemont House on Parnell Square North, an eighteenth-century stone-clad townhouse, next to the Dublin Writers Museum.

And so when all my little work is done
They'll say I came in Eighteen-seventy-one,
And died in Dublin. . . . What year will they write
For my poor passage to the stall of Night?

The answer came in the early morning of March 24, 1909, when Synge told his nurse, "It's no use fighting death any longer," then lay back and died.

The Dublin Writers Museum is a great center from which to explore literary Dublin.

Dublin Today: Rich and Varied

As if to make up for its sometimes tempestuous relationship with its writers, Dublin today has put its impressive literary heritage front and center. It is rightfully proud; perhaps no other city has quite as much claim to literary fame per square mile. Monuments to Irish history, both literary and political, are seemingly around every corner.

The best homage to Dublin's impressive literary pedigree is the ㉔ **Dublin Writers Museum, 18 Parnell Square.** This museum, housed in the eighteenth-century former residence of the Jameson family of whiskey fame, opened in 1991 and seeks to promote interest in the lives and works of Irish writers. The Irish Writers' Centre next door offers programs in support of working writers.

The two floors of the museum are crammed with things to see: artifacts, two rooms dedicated to Irish literary history, an art gallery, a bookshop, a café, and exhibition spaces. Among the items on display are early and first editions of well-known Irish books, Samuel Beckett's telephone, Lady Gregory's opera glasses, and James Joyce's piano.

This pub off Grafton Street is the starting place for the Dublin Literary Pub Crawl: two hours of literature, wit, and hard drinking.

For the more pedestrian literary fan, the ㉕ **Duke Pub, on Duke Street** just off Grafton Street, is the meeting place for Dublin's Literary Pub Crawl. The two-hour tour covers four to eight different pubs and features a staggering number of anecdotes and stories thrown in for good measure. The afternoon or evening jaunts are led by two trained actors who perform for thousands of visitors each year.

The National Block

For a more formal study of Irish history and culture, the National Block offers the National Gallery, the National

Library, the National Museum of Ireland–Natural History, the National Museum of Ireland–Archaeology and History, the State Heraldic Museum, and the Leinster House, all within a block of each other. The

Beloved by writers such as George Moore and William Butler Yeats, the National Library was a cultural anchor for the area south of the Liffey.

㉖ **National Gallery,** with its impressive collection of Jack Butler Yeats paintings, is on Merrion Square West between Oscar Wilde's house and Yeats's house, and next door to the Natural History Museum and the state buildings of the Dail, Ireland's legislative body.

The ㉗ **National Library,** on **Kildare Street,** is a particularly storied institution. During the years of the Revival, it served as an intellectual laboratory of sorts. W. K. Magee, who wrote under the name of John Eglinton and eventually became head librarian, was intimately connected with the Revival. He often walked with George Moore (who referred to him as the Thoreau of the suburbs) and contributed to many informal and published literary conversations in Dublin during the early twentieth century.

The library is notable for the major exhibition of Yeats artifacts and manuscripts that it has mounted since in May 2006. The exhibition is built on the extremely generous donations of Yeats's son and daughter-in-law, Michael and Grainne Yeats. Over the years, the couple presented the library with more than a thousand of Yeats's personal papers, and in 2002 they donated his library of three thousand volumes. Other highlights of the exhibition include digital touch-screen technology to "turn the pages" of the original works, an illuminated copy of "The Lake Isle of Innisfree" by Cuala Press, and the ceremonial Japanese sword given to Yeats in America.

A Continuing Tradition

In many ways, Dublin and Ireland itself have not changed significantly since the Literary Revival. Rocks that pop up in fields across the island are still incorporated into the intricate lace of stone walls that stretches as far as the eye can see. Three children might pass a chapel, crossing themselves while talking over the latest football and hurling scores, never missing a

This pedestrian bridge, which can swivel to let boat traffic pass, was dedicated to Sean O'Casey in 2005.

stride. And writers are still making international reputations in drama, poetry, and fiction.

However, much of that rock is now cemented into decorative stone walls fronting suburban mansions and starter houses. The three children passing the chapel may be a redhead, fair-skinned Irish girl walking between two Brazilian friends. And the dreamy poet making news today is likely to be a sunglasses-wearing rock star fronting one of the world's most famous rock bands.

That's not to say that Ireland has lost its literary touch. Poet Seamus Heaney was awarded the Nobel Prize in Literature in 1995. Contemporary Irish playwrights such as Brian Friel and Martin McDonagh continue to offer insightful and exciting theatre. In 1980 Heaney and Friel collaborated with artists including Stephen Rea and Seamus Deane to create the Field Day Theatre Company, a project that sought to address the political situation in Ireland through art without propaganda. In 1991, the project published the three-volume *Field Day Anthology of Irish Literature*. Although notably light on female writers, the anthology is an important contribution to the Irish literary canon.

Live theater continues to thrive in Ireland. The Abbey Theatre celebrated its hundredth anniversary with a series of lectures, revivals of its opening-night shows, and an exhibition of portraits from the Abbey at the National Gallery. The Druid Theatre Company of Galway celebrated its first thirty years by producing the entire Synge cycle. In addition, each October the Dublin Theatre Festival draws audiences from all over the world to its eclectic offerings.

In July 2005, the Dublin Docklands Development Authority named a pedestrian bridge over the River Liffey, from the Grand Canal Docks area to the North Wall Quay, the ㉓ Sean O'Casey Bridge in a ceremony led by Taoiseach (Prime Minister) Bertie Ahern.

For its part, the Irish Writers' Centre, operating from the same building as the Dublin Writers Museum, sponsors programs to support Ireland's many working writers. There are active summer schools and conferences dedicated to Irish writing from Sligo to Wicklow, and Irish films and music now account for much of what Yeats called "Ireland's gift of the imagination."

Timeline

February 24, 1852 — George Moore is born at Moore Hall in County Mayo.

March 15, 1852 — Isabella Augusta Persse—the future Lady Gregory—is born at Roxborough, near Loughrea in County Galway.

June 13, 1865 — William Butler Yeats is born in Sandymount, a suburb south of Dublin.

April 16, 1871 — John Millington Synge is born at Newton Little, Rathfarnham, a suburb of Dublin.

March 4, 1880 — Isabella Augusta Persse marries Sir William Gregory and becomes Lady Gregory.

March 30, 1880 — Sean O'Casey is born (as John Casey) in Dublin.

1881 — The Yeats family returns to Dublin after living in London for fourteen years. They move into Balscadden Cottage in Howth. Yeats attends Erasmus High School on Harcourt Street in Dublin.

May 1884 — Yeats enrolls at the Dublin Metropolitan School of Art and befriends George Russell.

1888 — Synge enters Trinity College, Dublin.

January 30, 1889 — Yeats first meets Maud Gonne. His infatuation with her will last his whole life.

October 6, 1891 — Irish nationalist politician Charles Stewart Parnell dies. He had earlier been driven from

Yeats lived in Howth for only two years but its seaside atmosphere affected his imagination long after.

power following the discovery of his affair with Katharine O'Shea. His death inspires many Irish nationalists to turn from political to cultural activities.

March 1892 — Sir William Gregory dies, leaving Lady Gregory a widow.

November 25, 1892 — Douglas Hyde gives an address to the National Literary Society titled "The Necessity for De-Anglicizing Ireland," which serves as the foundation for the Gaelic League, created the following year.

December 1893 — Yeats publishes *The Celtic Twilight*.

November 1894 — Yeats stays with the Gore-Booth family at Lissadell in Sligo.

August 1896 — Yeats and Arthur Symons visit Edward Martyn at Tullira Castle, where they meet Lady Gregory.

December 21, 1896 — Yeats meets J. M. Synge in Paris and advises him to visit the Aran Islands.

July 1897 — Yeats spends his first summer at Coole Park. Yeats, Lady Gregory, and Edward Martyn found the Irish Literary Theatre.

May 10–June 25, 1898 — Synge visits the Aran Islands.

May 8, 1899 — The Irish Literary Theatre stages its first plays, Martyn's *The Heather Field* and Yeats's *The Countess Cathleen*, in the Antient Concert Rooms in Dublin. J. M. Synge is in the audience.

October 21, 1901 — The Irish Literary Theatre stages Douglas Hyde's play *Casadh an tSugan* in Gaelic at the Gaiety Theatre.

Brightly colored front doors have long been a feature of Dublin. Some people claim they were originally painted to help people find their own homes after long evenings in the pubs.

April 2, 1902 — Yeats and Gregory stage *Cathleen Ni Houlihan* with Maud Gonne in the title role at St. Teresa's Total Abstinence Hall on Clarendon Street.

May 19, 1902 — George Moore produces Douglas Hyde's *An Tincear agus an tSidheog* (*The Tinker and the Fairy*) in his backyard on Ely Street.

March 14, 1903 — Lady Gregory's first play, *Twenty-Five*, is performed at the Molesworth Hall by the Irish National Theatre Company

October 8, 1903 — Synge's *In the Shadow of the Glen* is performed at the Molesworth Theatre.

November 1903 — Yeats embarks on his first U.S. lecture tour.

August 20, 1904 — The Irish National Theatre Society receives a license to operate the Abbey Theatre.

December 27, 1904 — The Abbey Theatre opens with *Cathleen Ni Houlihan*, Yeats's *On Baile's Strand*, and Gregory's *Spreading the News*.

September 22, 1905 — Synge is elected a director of the Irish National Theatre Society

January 26, 1907 — J. M. Synge's *The Playboy of the Western World* opens at the Abbey Theatre, causing riots.

March 9, 1907 — Lady Gregory's *The Rising of the Moon* is first produced at the Abbey.

March 24, 1909 — J. M. Synge dies of Hodgkin's disease in Dublin.

January 18, 1912 — The Abbey Theatre Company is

arrested in Philadelphia prior to a performance of *The Playboy of the Western World*.

March 1916 — Yeats publishes the first installment of his autobiography, *Reveries over Childhood and Youth*.

April 24, 1916 — On Easter morning, Fenian rebels take control of the General Post Office as well as other locations around Dublin. They hold these positions before eventually surrendering to the British Army on April 29.

March 28, 1917 — Yeats prints twenty-five copies of his poem "Easter, 1916" for friends but does not publish it in its entirety until 1920.

May 16, 1917 — The Congested Districts Board officially transfers the title for Thoor Ballylee into Yeats's name.

October 21, 1917 — Yeats marries Georgina Hyde-Lees.

January 23, 1918 — Robert Gregory, Lady Gregory's only son, dies in World War I.

January 21, 1919 — The Irish Republican Army kills two policemen in County Tipperary, contributing to the beginning of the Anglo-Irish War.

March 18, 1919 — Lady Gregory plays the title role in *Cathleen Ni Houlihan* at the Abbey Theatre.

December 6, 1922 — The Irish Free State is established.

December 11, 1922 — Yeats joins the Irish Free State Senate and serves until 1928.

April 12, 1923 — Sean O'Casey's *The Shadow of a Gunman* debuts at the Abbey Theatre.

December 10, 1923 — Yeats receives the Nobel Prize in Literature in Stockholm.

October 8, 1924 — Lady Gregory's family house, Roxborough, burns down.

February 8, 1926 — Sean O'Casey's *The Plough and the Stars* opens at the Abbey, causing riots over its perceived antinationalist stance.

April 1, 1927 — Coole Park is sold to the Irish Ministry of Lands and Agriculture.

May 22, 1932 — Lady Gregory dies at Coole Park.

January 21, 1933 — George Moore dies in London.

January 28, 1939 — Yeats dies of a heart attack in the South of France. According to his wishes, he is buried temporarily in France until the media furor dies down. Unfortunately, due to World War II, he cannot be re-interred in Sligo until 1948.

1941 — Coole Park is demolished.

September 18, 1964 — Sean O'Casey dies in Devon, England.

June 20, 1965 — Thoor Ballylee is renovated and opened as a museum.

Notes

Chapter 1

3: Information on Ireland's history is from Máire and Conor Cruise O'Brien, *Ireland: A Concise History* (New York: Thames and Hudson, 1985); *The Encyclopedia of Ireland*, ed. Ciaran Brady (New York: Oxford University Press, 2000); and R. F. Foster, *The Oxford Illustrated History of Ireland* (New York: Oxford University Press, 1989).

8: "Parnell was the first . . .": Ulick O'Connor, *All the Olympians* (New York: Atheneum, 1984), 4.

8: "set the style . . .": O'Connor, *All the Olympians*, 115.

9: Douglas Hyde, "My Grief on the Sea," in *Irish Literature: A Reader*, ed. Maureen O'Rourke Murphy and James MacKillop (Syracuse: Syracuse University Press, 1987), 134.

10: "provide the free Ireland . . .": Robert Tracy, "General Introduction," *The Aran Islands and Other Writings*, ed. Robert Tracy (New York: Random House, 1962).

11: Information on Joyce and the Irish Literary Revival can be found in R. F. Foster, *W. B. Yeats: A Life—The Apprentice Mage* (Oxford: Oxford University Press, 1997), 276.

14: "here beside a little stream . . .": as quoted in R. F. Foster, *W. B. Yeats: A Life—The Arch-Poet* (Oxford: Oxford University Press, 2003), 243.

Chapter 2

18: Information about Lady Gregory's time at Coole comes from Lady Augusta Gregory, *Selected Writings* (London: Penguin Books, 1995); Lady Augusta Gregory, *Seventy Years: Being the Autobiography of Lady Gregory* (New York: Macmillan, 1974); Colm Toibin, *Lady Gregory's Toothbrush* (London: Pan Macmillan, 2002); Mary Lou Kohfeldt, *Lady Gregory: The Woman behind the Irish Renaissance* (New York: Atheneum, 1985); and Colin Smythe, *A Guide to Coole Park, Co. Galway* (Buckinghamshire, UK: Colin Smythe, 2003).

20: "At the midnight . . .": Gregory, *Selected Writings*, 3.

21: Anecdote about the Christmas books comes from Kohfeldt, *Lady Gregory*, 29.

21: "a house . . .": Gregory, *Selected Writings*, 28.

21: "Left Dublin at . . .": as quoted in Sister Mary De Lourdes Fahy, "Lady Gregory—A Local Habitation and a Name," *Lady Gregory Autumn Gatherings: Reflections at Coole*, ed. Sean Toibin (Galway: Lady Gregory Autumn Gathering, 2000), 5.

22: Information about the Coole estate and Sir William Gregory's ancestors comes from Kohfeldt, *Lady Gregory*, 49.

22: "Yet Roxborough . . .": Gregory, *Selected Writings*, 29.

23: "a plainly dressed woman . . .": William Butler Yeats, *Autobiographies*, ed. William H. O'Donnell and Douglas N. Archibald (New York: Scribner, 1999), 293.

23: "if you get our . . .": as quoted in Kohfeldt, *Lady Gregory*, 109.

24: "There seemed to be . . .": as quoted in Gregory, *Seventy Years*, 378.

25: "He hadn't been . . .": Sean O'Casey, *The Sean O'Casey Reader: Plays, Autobiographies, Opinions*, ed. Brooks Atkinson (New York: St. Martin's Press, 1968), 764.

25: "a savage land . . .": as quoted on www.goireland.com.

25: Yeats's poetry is from *The Poems*, ed. Richard J. Finneran (New York: Macmillan, 1989).

26: "the Seven Woods . . .": O'Casey, *The Sean O'Casey Reader*, 765.

27: "And on the great . . .": as quoted in Smythe, *A Guide to Coole Park*, 19.

27: "Today Augusta made . . .": as quoted in Foster, *The Apprentice Mage*, 247.

27: "We actually watched . . .": Anne Gregory, *Me and Nu: Childhood at Coole* (Buckinghamshire, UK: Colin Smythe, 1970), 63.

27: "But alas! . . .": Gregory, as quoted in Smythe, *A Guide to Coole Park*, 19.

28: "I was to . . .": Yeats, *Autobiographies*, 291.

29: Information on Lady Gregory's rent comes from Kohfeldt, *Lady Gregory*, 290.

31: "I feel it . . .": as quoted in Toibin, *Lady Gregory's Toothbrush*, 25.

31: "When I began . . .": Lady Augusta Gregory, *Cuchulain of Muirthemne*, www. Gutenberg.org.

33: Information on Yeats and Hyde's visits to Tullira Castle come from O'Connor, *All the Olympians*, and Foster, *The Apprentice Mage*.

34: "As soon as . . .": quoted in O'Connor, *All the Olympians*, 124.

34: "I dream in Irish": as quoted in Declan Kiberd, *Inventing Ireland: The Literature of the Modern Nation* (Cambridge, Mass.: Harvard University Press, 1995), 138.

34: "The garden was full . . .": Gregory, *Our Irish Theatre*, 4.

34: "And then one . . .": Gregory, *Selected Writings*, 46.

35: "We propose . . .": Gregory, *Our Irish Theatre*, 8–9.

36: Information on Raftery, including the anecdote about receiving poetic talent from the fairies, is from Joe Solan, "Raftery and His Times," unpublished.

37: "Drink Raftery, and . . .": Gregory, *Kiltartan Poetry Book*, www.gutenberg.com.

37: "There is the old . . .": Yeats, *The Celtic Twilight*, www.gutenberg.com.

37: Much of the information about Thoor Ballylee and Yeats's time there comes from Mary Hanley and Liam Miller, *Thoor Ballylee: Home of William Butler Yeats* (Dublin: Dolmen Press, 1977); and Foster, *The Apprentice Mage*.

39: "We are settled here . . .": W. B. Yeats, *The Letters of W. B. Yeats*, ed. Wade Allen (London: Rupert Hart-Davis, 1954), 680.

39: "It is a great . . .": Yeats, *The Letters of W. B. Yeats*, 683.

40: Information on the blowing up of the Thoor Ballylee bridge comes from Foster, *The Arch-Poet*, 214–15.

40: "I have all the thought . . .": as quoted in Foster, *The Arch-Poet*, 23.

40: Pound's "Ballyphallus" quotation is from a letter to John Quinn, June 1, 1920, as quoted in Foster, *The Arch-Poet*, 84.

41: "The ruin has . . .": D. J. Gordon and Ian Fletcher, as quoted in Hanley and Miller, *Thoor Ballylee*, 26.

42: "neither O nor . . .": as quoted on wikipedia.com.

42: "Hangings were daily . . .": Diana Farrell Serbe, "A Tour

of Galway—The Glorious Past and Swinging Present," inmamaskitchen.com.

Chapter 3

45: "These islands were . . .": O'Connor, *All the Olympians*, 123.

46: "I first saw . . .": Gregory, *Our Irish Theatre*, 114.

47: "I said 'Give . . .' ": W. B. Yeats, "Preface to *The Well of the Saints*," *Essays and Introductions* (New York: Macmillan, 1961), 299.

48: "Synge learned in . . .": Robert Tracy, "Preface," John Millington Synge, *The Aran Islands* (New York: Vintage Books, 1962), xiii.

49–59: All quotations by Synge are from *The Aran Islands*.

55: "He spoke seldom. . .": Oliver St. John Gogarty, *As I Was Going Down Sackville Street* (New York: Reynal & Hitchcock, 1937), 293.

Chapter 4

61: Information on County Mayo geography and history is from www.mayo-ireland.ie, as is some of the information about Moore Hall and the Moore family. Additional information on the Moore family, including the quotation from George Henry Moore, comes from www.castlebar.ie/imagemayo/moore.htm.

63: "on a pleasant . . .": George Moore, *Hail and Farewell* (Buckinghamshire, UK: Colin Smythe, 1985), 468.

63: "ratlike faces with . . .": Moore, *Hail and Farewell*, 293.

64: Much of the information about George Moore's early involvement in the Irish Literary Revival and some of the critical analysis, including quotations, come from Richard Allen Cave's introduction to the Colin Smythe edition of *The Untilled Field*. The quotations from Moore's preface are from the same volume.

64: "Is it my . . .": Manet, as quoted in O'Connor, *All the Olympians*, 35.

64: Accounts of Yeats's plan for *Diarmuid and Grania* appear in O'Connor, *All the Olympians*, 196; and Moore, *Hail and Farewell*, 248.

65: "Moore's preoccupation . . .": Richard Allen Cave,

"Introduction," *The Untilled Field,* ed. Richard Allen Cave (Buckinghamshire, UK: Colin Smythe, 2000), xxiv.

65: "The policy of . . .": Moore, *The Untilled Field,* 101.

66: *The Untilled Field* sets . . .": Cave, *The Untilled Field,* xiv.

66: "We all did . . .": Moore, *The Untilled Field,* xxix.

66: "Lady Gregory will translate . . .": Moore, *Hail and Farewell,* 248.

66: "Story followed story . . .": Moore, *Hail and Farewell,* 347.

66: "paint the portrait . . .": Moore, *The Untilled Field,* xxix.

67: "It seemed to . . .": Moore, *The Untilled Field,* xxxii.

68: "It is a gaunt . . .": Richard Jones, www.haunted-britain.com.

68: "I was now . . .": Yeats, *Autobiographies,* 106.

69: "He forsook . . .": Derek Mahon, "Euphorion in Ely Place," www.oreillydesign.com/morehall/mahon.html.

70: "Killedan the village . . .": Raftery, from http://www.museumsofmayo.com/Kiltimagh2.htm.

70: Information on Killala and the uprising is from www.irelandwest.ie.

70: "He often tells me . . .": Synge, *The Aran Islands,* 61.

73: All quotes from John Millington Synge, *The Playboy of the Western World,* are from www.gutenberg.com.

Chapter 5

75: "Years afterwards, when . . .": Yeats, *Autobiographies,* 49.

75: "Drumcliff and Rosses . . .": Yeats, *The Celtic Twilight,* www.gutenberg.com.

77: "sometimes because I . . .": Yeats, *Autobiographies,* 206.

78: The anecdote about Yeats and his cousin out on the water comes from Yeats, *Autobiographies,* 85–86.

78: "a little sea-dividing . . .": Yeats, *The Celtic Twilight,* www.gutenberg.com.

79: "chokeful of ghosts . . .": Yeats, *The Celtic Twilight,* www.gutenberg.com.

79: "believe whatever had . . .": Yeats, *Autobiographies,* 89.

79: "When I look . . .": Yeats, *Autobiographies,* 72.

80: "Indeed, there are . . .": Yeats, *The Celtic Twilight,* www.gutenberg.com.

80: "is but her . . .": Yeats, *Autobiographies,* 84.

80: "There are some . . .": Yeats, *Autobiographies,* 207.

80: Information regarding Lissadell House and the Gore-Booth sisters comes from www.lissadellhouse.com.

81: "an exceedingly impressive . . .": Yeats, *The Letters of W. B. Yeats,* 240.

82: "I told . . .": Yeats, *Autobiographies,* 85.

82: "I thought that . . .": Yeats, *Autobiographies,* 85.

83: Information on the People's Millennium Forests Project comes from www.millenniumforests.com.

83: "What makes the . . .": Kiberd, *Inventing Ireland,* 4.

84: "I still had . . .": Yeats, *Autobiographies,* 139.

87: "A little north . . .": Yeats, *The Celtic Twilight,* www.gutenberg.com.

88: Information on Drumcliff Church is from http://drumcliffe.elphin.anglican.org/history.shtml.

89: "The house was . . .": Yeats, *Autobiographies,* 41.

Chapter 6

93: Synge's poetry comes from J. M. Synge, *Synge's Collected Works,* volume 1, *Poetry,* ed. Robin Skelton (New York: Random House, 1935).

95: "When I was writing . . .": Synge, preface to *The Playboy of the Western World,* www.gutenberg.com.

97: "Come along with . . .": Synge, *The Complete Plays,* 117.

97: "The coffin was . . .": Synge, *The Aran Islands,* 128.

97: "It's little need . . .": Synge, *The Complete Plays,* 209.

100: Information on the Irish tinkers can be found at http://ac.uk/collections/gypsy/travel.htm.

103: Information on the Military Road can be found at www.glencree-dfr.ie/glencree_history.htm.

Chapter 7

109: Information on Yeats's time in Howth comes from Foster,

The Apprentice Mage, 27–28.

109: "Our house for . . .": Yeats, *Autobiographies*, 77–78.

109: "To approach the . . .": Yeats, *The Celtic Twilight*, www.gutenberg.com.

109: "These H—— spirits . . .": Yeats, *The Celtic Twilight*, www.gutenberg.com.

110: Information on Yeats's time at Erasmus High School comes from Yeats, *Autobiographies*, and W. J. R. Wallace, *Faithful to Our Trust: A History of the Erasmus Smith Trust and the High School, Dublin* (Dublin: The Columba Press, 2004), 141–47.

110: "I found an . . .": Yeats, *Autobiographies*, 74.

111: "What could . . .": Yeats, *Autobiographies*, 75.

111: Some of the information about George Russell, Mountjoy Square, J. M. Synge, and Ely Place is from goireland.com.

112: "wild red hair . . .": Yeats, *Rosa Alchemica*, www.gutenberg.com.

113: Information about the formation of the Irish theater, especially quotes from Lady Gregory and the poem by Lionel Johnson, can be found in Gregory, *Our Irish Theatre*; Foster, *The Apprentice Mage*; and O'Connor, *All the Olympians*.

114: "show that . . .": Gregory, *Our Irish Theatre*, www.gutenberg.com.

114: "If the plays . . .": Moore, *Hail and Farewell*, 93–94.

115: "twenty brainless, beardless . . .": as quoted in Gregory, *Our Irish Theatre*, www.gutenberg.com.

116: "This time we . . .": Gregory, *Our Irish Theatre*, www.gutenberg.com.

116: "That day she . . .": Yeats, *Autobiographies*, 120.

118: "a huge cart-wheel . . ." and "the father and mother . . .": as quoted in Toibin, *Lady Gregory's Toothbrush*, 55.

119: "In writing . . .": Synge, "Preface to *The Playboy of the Western World*," www.gutenberg.com.

120: "It's Pegeen Mike . . .": Synge, *The Playboy of the Western World*, www.gutenberg.com.

120: "It is better . . .": Synge, as quoted in Ben Levitas, "Synge and the Dublin of His Time," http://syngecycle .com/synge/synge-and-the-dublin-of-his-time.html.

121: Information on the Abbey's American tour is from Christopher Fitz-Simon, *The Abbey Theatre* (London: Thames and Hudson, 2003), 42.

121: "Boston is a . . .": Gregory, *Our Irish Theatre*, www.gutenberg.com.

121: "No, our countrymen . . .": Gregory, *Our Irish Theatre*, www.gutenberg.com.

121: Information on Eugene O'Neill's reaction to the Abbey tour in New York, including quotation, is from Fintan O'Toole, "Synge's Influence," http://syngecycle .com/synge/synges-influence-

121: Information on the riots at *The Plough and the Stars*, including the quotations from Yeats, is from David Granville, "The 1926 Abbey Rising," www.irishdemocrat.co.uk/features/ the-1926-abbey-rising/; O'Casey, *The Sean O'Casey Reader*, 779–81; and Foster, *The Arch-Poet*, 305–6.

126: "The one house . . .": Yeats, *Autobiographies*, 193.

127: "A figure with . . .": Gogarty, *As I Was Going Down Sackville Street*, 302.

128: Information on Yeats's time at Merrion Square including information about the Cuala Press, can be found in Foster, *The Arch-Poet*, 210.

128: "It puts back . . .": Yeats to Lady Gregory, February 23, 1923, and March 9, 1922, Berg collection (as quoted in Foster, *The Arch-Poet*, 210).

128: Information on the night Yeats won the Nobel Prize is from the author's interview with Michael Yeats.

128: "Ricketts watercolours . . .": Foster, *The Arch-Poet*, 224.

129: Information on Synge's death can be found in Moore, *Hail and Farewell*, 560–61; and Robin Skelton, ed. *Synge and His World* (New York: Viking Press, 1971), 130.

130: Information on Hugh Lane and the National Gallery comes from www.hughlane.ie/about/hugh.shtml.

For Further Reading

Writings by Members of the Revival

Gregory, Isabelle Augusta. *Lady Gregory's Diaries: 1892–1902.* Edited by James Pethica. New York: Oxford University Press, 1996.

———. *Our Irish Theatre.* www.gutenberg.com.

———. *Selected Writings.* Edited by Lucy McDiarmid and Maureen Waters. London: Penguin, 1995.

———. *Seventy Years.* Edited by Colin Smythe. New York: Macmillan, 1974.

Moore, George. *Hail and Farewell!* Edited by Richard Allen Cave. Buckinghamshire, UK: Colin Smythe, 2003.

———. *The Untilled Field.* Edited by Richard Allen Cave. Buckinghamshire, UK: Colin Smythe, 2000.

O'Casey, Sean. *The Sean O'Casey Reader: Plays, Autobiographies, Opinions.* Edited by Brooks Atkinson. New York: St. Martin's Press, 1968.

Synge, J. M. *The Complete Plays of John M. Synge.* New York: Random House, 1935.

———. *Travels in Wicklow, West Kerry, and Connemara.* London: Serif, 2005.

Yeats, William Butler. *Autobiographies.* Edited by William H. O'Donnell and Douglas N. Archibald. New York: Scribner, 1999.

———. *The Poems.* Edited by Richard J. Finneran. New York: Macmillan, 1989.

Biographies and Critical Studies

Cahill, Susan, ed. *For the Love of Ireland: A Literary Companion for Readers and Travelers.* New York: Ballentine Books, 2001.

Cruise O'Brien, Máire and Conor. *Ireland: A Concise History.* New York: Thames and Hudson, 1997.

Fallis, Richard. *The Irish Renaissance.* Syracuse, N.Y.: Syracuse University Press, 1977.

Fitz-Simon, Christopher. *The Abbey Theatre.* London: Thames and Hudson, 2003.

Foster, R. F. *W. B. Yeats: A Life—The Apprentice Mage.* Oxford: Oxford University Press, 1998.

———. *W. B. Yeats: A Life—The Arch-Poet.* Oxford: Oxford University Press, 2003.

Hanley, Mary, and Liam Miller. *Thoor Ballylee: Home of William Butler Yeats.* Buckinghamshire, UK: Colin Smythe, 1995.

Igoe, Vivien. *A Literary Guide to Dublin: Writers in Dublin, Literary Associations and Anecdotes.* London: Methuen London, 1994.

Kiberd, Declan. *Inventing Ireland: The Literature of the Modern Nation.* Cambridge, Mass.: Harvard University Press, 1995.

Kohfeldt, Mary Lou. *Lady Gregory: The Woman behind the Irish Renaissance.* New York: Atheneum, 1985.

O'Connor, Ulick. *All the Olympians.* New York: Atheneum, 1984.

Skelton, Robin. *J. M. Synge and His World.* New York: Viking Press, 1971.

Smythe, Colin. *A Guide to Coole Park.* Buckinghamshire, UK: Colin Smythe, 2003.

Tobin, Sean, ed. *Lady Gregory Autumn Gatherings: Reflections at Coole.* Galway: Lady Gregory Autumn Gathering, 2000.

Toibin, Colm. *Lady Gregory's Toothbrush.* London: Pan Macmillan, 2003.

Web Resources

Beyond Ben Bulben. Australian Yeats Society. www.benbulben.net.

Collected Poems of W. B. Yeats. California State University, Northridge. www.csun.edu/~hceng029/yeats/collectedpoems .html.

Dublin Theatre Festival. www.dublintheatrefestival.com.

Dublin Tourist Office. www.visitdublin.ie.

Dublin Writers Museum. www.writersmuseum.com.

GoIreland. www.goireland.com.

International Association for the Study of Irish Literature (IASIL). www.iasl.org.

Irish Literary Collections Portal. Emory University Special Collections. http://irishliterature.library.emory. edu/doc-geninfo.

Literary Traveler. www.literarytraveler.com.

National Library of Ireland. www.nli.ie

Project Gutenberg. www.gutenberg.com.

Sligo Zone. www.sligozone.net.

Yeats Society Sligo. www.yeats-sligo.com/index.html.

Index

Credits

Text

Lines from "Under Ben Bulben" reprinted with the permission of Scribner, an imprint of Simon & Schuster Adult Publishing Group, from THE COLLECTED POEMS OF W.B. YEATS, VOLUME I: THE POEMS, Revised edited by Richard J. Finneran. Copyright © 1940 by Geogie Yeats; copyright renewed © 1968 by Bertha Geogie Yeats, Michael Butler Yeats & Anne Yeats. All rights reserved.

Lines from "Towards the Break of Day" and "Easter 1916" reprinted with the permiSSion of Scribner, an imprint of Simon & Schuster Adult Publishing Group, from THE COLLECTED POEMS OF W.B. YEATS, VOLUME I: THE POEMS, Revised edited by Richard J. Finneran. Copyright © 1924 by The Macmillan Company; copyright renewed © 1952 by Bertha Georgie Yeats. All rights reserved.

Lines from "Coole Park 1929" reprinted with the permission of Scribner, an imprint of Simon & Schuster Adult Publishing Group, from THE COLLECTED POEMS OF W.B. YEATS, VOLUME I: THE POEMS, Revised edited by Richard J. Finneran. Copyright © 1933 by The Macmillan Company; copyright renewed © 1961 by Bertha Georgie Yeats. All rights reserved.

Lines from "The Tower" reprinted with the permission of Scribner, an imprint of Simon & Schuster Adult Publishing Group, from THE COLLECTED POEMS OF W.B. YEATS, VOLUME I: THE POEMS, Revised edited by Richard J. Finneran. Copyright © 1928 by The Macmillan Company; copyright renewed © 1956 by Bertha Georgie Yeats. All rights reserved.

Lines from "To Ireland in the Coming Times," "The Wild Swans at Coole," "In Memory of Major Robert Gregory," "The Shadowy Waters," "The Fiddler of Dooney" reprinted with the permission of Scribner, an imprint of Simon & Schuster Adult Publishing Group, from THE COLLECTED POEMS OF W.B. YEATS, VOLUME I: THE POEMS,

Revised edited by Richard J. Finneran. (New York: Scribner, 1997). All rights reserved.

Art

Image on page 153 is courtesy of Betsy Archer.

The following are courtesy of Colin Smythe Publishers: images on pages 18, 20, 23, 24, 29, 33, and 39.

Image on page 83 is courtesy of the Concord Free Public Library.

Image on page 91 (statue) is courtesy of Alison D'Arcy.

Image on page 127 is courtesy of Emory University.

Image on page 54 is courtesy of Inis Meain Knitwear.

Images on pages 6, 42, and 72 are from Istock.com.

The following are from the U.S. Library of Congress: images on front cover (LC-DIG-ppmsc-09883), page 10 and back cover (LC-USZ62-104093), page 11 (LC-USZ62-115886), page 98 (LC-USZ62-93720), page 114 (LC-USZ62-103919), and page 116 (LC-USZ62-97179)

Image on page 49 is courtesy of Limerick Museum.

The following are from the Mander & Mitchenson Theatre Collection: images on pages 4, 115, and 117.

Image on page 63 (Coranna) is courtesy of Mayo Ireland Ltd.

Image on 71 is courtesy of Gareth McCormack.

Image on page 64 is from the Metropolitan Museum of Art, H. O. Havermeyer Collection, Bequest of Mrs. H. O. Havermeyer, 1929 (29.100.55). Photograph © 1990, The Metropolitan Museum of Art.

Image on page 12 is from the Michigan State University Theatre Archive.

The following are courtesy of the National Gallery of Ireland: image on page 9 and back cover, *William Butler Yeats* by John Yeats; image on page 112, *AE* by John Butler Yeats; and image on page 122, *Yeats and the Irish Theatre* by Edmund Dulac.

The following are courtesy of the National Library of Ireland: images on pages 63 (Moore Hall), 81, 99, 118, 124, and 125.

Image on page 36 is from the Henry W. and Albert A. Berg Collection of English and American Literature, The New York Public Library, Astor, Lenox and Tilden Foundations.

The following are courtesy of Old Images of Ireland: images on pages 70, 77, 94, and 100.

Image on page 69 (headstone) is courtesy of O'Reilly Designs. Image on page 133 is courtesy of Aidan O'Rourke.

Image on page 69 (Renvyle House) is courtesy of Renvyle House.

Image on page 111, view of the cloakroom interior, The High School, Dublin, ca. 1880s. Courtesy of the Board of Governors of the Schools founded by Erasmus Smith Esq. Dublin.

Image on pages 25 and 60 are courtesy of T. J. Tierney, www.goldenirishlight.com.

Images on pages 22 and 79 are courtesy of Michael Yeats.

All other images are in the author's or publisher's collections or in the public domain.

About the Author

R. Todd Felton is a writer and photographer specializing in literary travel. He is the author of the ArtPlace book *A Journey into the Transcendentalists' New England* and has written for *The Massachusetts Sierran*, *Our Turn II*, *WMA Responds*, the Amherst NPR affiliate, www.realtfs.com, and *The Automobile Traveler*. His photographs have been featured in an exhibition at the Fruitlands Museum in Massachusetts and the 2005 Focusing on the Range competition. Todd lives in Amherst, Massachusetts, with his wife and sons, Tim and Liam.

About the ArtPlace Series

This book is part of the ArtPlace series published by Roaring Forties Press. Each book in the series explores how a renowned artist and a world-famous city or area helped to define and inspire each other. ArtPlace volumes are intended to stimulate both eye and mind, offering a rich mix of art and photography, history and biography, ideas and information. While the books can be used by tourists to navigate and illuminate their way through cityscapes and landscapes, they can also be enjoyed by armchair travelers in search of an engrossing and revealing story.

Other titles in the series include *A Journey into Dorothy Parker's New York*, *A Journey into Steinbeck's California*, *A Journey into the Transcendentalists' New England*, *A Journey into Matisse's South of France*, and *A Journey into Flaubert's Normandy*.

Visit Roaring Forties Press's website, www.roaringfortiespress.com, for details of these and other titles, as well as to learn about upcoming author tours, readings, media appearances, and special events and offers. Visitors to the website may also send comments and questions to the authors of ArtPlace series books.

A Journey into Ireland's Literary Revival

This book is set in Goudy and Futura; the display type is Futura Condensed. The interior and cover of the book were designed by Jeff Urbancic, who also made up the pages. Kim Rusch designed the maps. Nigel Quinney and Sherri Schultz edited the text, which was proofread by Karen Stough and indexed by Jan Williams.